POSITIVE EATING,
A GUIDE TO EVERYDAY HEALTH & NUTRITION
WITH EASY-TO-COOK RECIPES

Popular Prakashan
www.popularprakashan.com

Published by Harsha Bhatkal
for Popular Prakashan Pvt. Ltd.
301, Mahalaxmi Chambers
22, Bhulabhai Desai Road
Mumbai - 400026
www.popularprakashan.com

First Published 2018

(4490)
ISBN 978-81-7991-931-6

Design & Art Direction by Isha Jhunjhunwala

Printed by
Saurabh Printers (P) Ltd.
Plot No. 67, A-68, Ecotech, Ext. I
Kasna, Greater Noida-201306 (UP)

Acknowledgements

This book would not have been possible without the encouragement from my son Udit. His persistence, patience and support has kept me going.

I am eternally thankful to Isha and Muskaan who have worked hard and enthusiastically to make this book a reality.

I would also like to thank my husband Ravi for tasting all the dishes, my son Dhruv for editing the book, and my family for taking pride and interest in my venture.

Lastly, I wish to thank my teacher Niyati Parekh, who has been a constant source of inspiration and has nurtured my love for nutrition.

CONTENTS

Radhika Toshniwal, the author

Radhika Toshniwal has been practicing nutrition for over 15 years. She is a mother of two, and a fitness enthusiast. At the age of 40, she was inspired to study how food affects our body and mind. Her passion for nutrition led her to experiment with healthy cooking. She replaced ingredients in everyday recipes with healthier options, always staying true to her belief that food should be simple, healthy and at the same time, yummy.

Often, the topics on which she writes are influenced by the people she meets and their health concerns. The idea of writing a book came from the encouragement from the readers of her Facebook page on nutrition. There is nothing like capturing the essence of over 10 years of digital publication into a coffee table book that can occupy living rooms and kitchens and help people to build healthy eating habits so as to lead more nourished lives.

During her travels, she enjoys tasting local food, imbibing new flavours, and experimenting with foreign ingredients. Some of these recipes have been included in this book.

How to use this book:

Almost all recipes take between 10-20 minutes to prepare and have been tried, tested and modified especially for you!

Below is a key explaining the icons used in the book:

V VEGAN

GF GLUTEN-FREE

HIGH FIBRE

HIGH PROTEIN

LACTOSE-FREE

ALKALIZERS

FOODS THAT NEUTRALISE ACIDITY

KALE

(from left to right)

PUMPKIN & KALE SALAD

KALE FRITTERS

Kale,
the new trendy vegetable

Kale is a vegetable with green or purple curly leaves, which has a strong and distinct flavour. It is very high in fibre, Vitamin A, Vitamin C and Vitamin K. It has antioxidant and anti-inflammatory properties.

One cup of kale is just 33 calories, and it's packed with lots of nutrients. Its combination of protein and fibre leaves you feeling full for much longer than typical greens. Kale reduces the risk of cancer, detoxifies the blood, lowers cholesterol and lowers blood pressure. Diabetics and asthmatics can benefit greatly from including it as a regular part of their diet.

Have it as a cold pressed juice, salad or as a vegetable! Or finely chop it and add it to soups, sauces, eggs and even smoothies.

POSITIVE TAKEAWAYS

+ High in fibre
+ Antioxidant and anti-inflammatory
+ Detoxifies blood
+ Good for diabetics & heart patients

KALE FRITTERS

PREPARATION TIME : UNDER 10 MINUTES
MAKES ABOUT 5-8 FRITTERS (LOW GLYCEMIC INDEX)

2 cups of kale leaves
1 1/2 inch ginger, finely chopped
1/2 teaspoon ground cumin
1/2 teaspoon onion powder
1/2 teaspoon garlic powder
Salt to taste
1/4 teaspoon cayenne pepper or red chilli powder
Ground black pepper to taste

1/2 cup cooked pearl barley (quinoa, dalia, oats, poha, can replace barley)

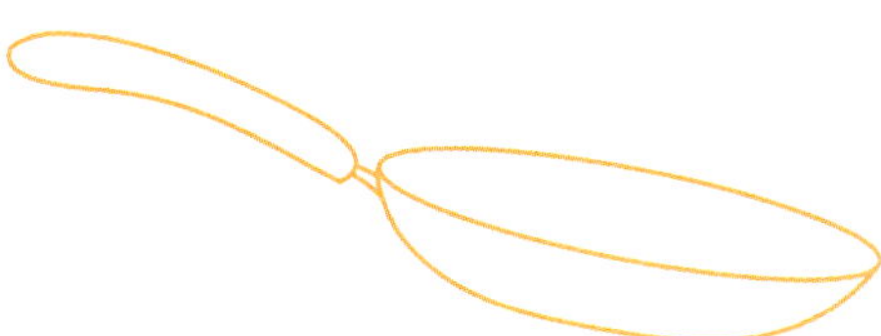

Add kale leaves, ginger, cumin powder, onion powder, garlic powder, salt, cayenne pepper and black pepper powder in a food processor and process till all the kale is chopped up. Transfer it into a medium bowl. (Do not over process, since the kale should not become a paste/purée. It should look like chopped leaves.)

Add pearl barley and mix well.

Divide the mixture into equal portions and shape them into flat fritters.

Heat a non-stick pan and grill the fritters, turning sides, till equally done on both sides. Serve hot.

Note:
Each cereal provides a different nutrient. Pearl barley is very low in glycemic index, quinoa is high in protein, broken wheat and oats are high in fibre and beaten rice binds best.
To this recipe one can further add protein in the form of cottage cheese or green peas.

PUMPKIN & KALE SALAD

PREPARATION TIME : UNDER 10 MINUTES
SERVES : 4

V GF

$^{3}/_{4}$ cup raw unsalted pumpkin seeds
Salt to taste
Pinch of cayenne pepper or red chilli powder
1 tablespoon maple syrup or honey

4 cups peeled, seeded, and 1-inch cubes of squash or pumpkin
2 garlic cloves, minced
1 tablespoon minced fresh rosemary (Thyme, oregano, basil or ginger can replace rosemary)
4 cups washed and torn kale leaves

Heat a non-stick pan, add the pumpkin seeds, salt and cayenne pepper powder and sauté till fragrant and golden brown.

Take pumpkin seeds in a bowl, add maple syrup, and toss well.

Put squash/pumpkin cubes, $^{1}/_{3}$ cup water, a little salt, garlic, rosemary into a large non-stick pan. Cover and cook on high heat till they are tender and the water evaporates. Uncover pan and continue to cook, stirring frequently, until the squash/pumpkin cubes are golden brown. Do not overcook in order to evaporate the moisture as over-cooking destroys nutrients.

Add kale and cook until it is wilted. Transfer into a serving dish, sprinkle some pumpkin seeds and serve hot or cold.

KALE SALAD WITH MISO MUSHROOM OMELETTE

PREPARATION TIME : UNDER 10 MINUTES
SERVES : 4

Lemon Chilli Vinaigrette

1/3 cup freshly squeezed lemon juice
1 garlic clove, finely minced
1/2 teaspoon salt
2 tablespoons extra virgin olive oil
1 teaspoon chilli oil or chilli sauce
2 teaspoons Dijon mustard powder
2 teaspoons honey
Freshly ground black peppercorns

To make the salad dressing, mix together lemon juice, garlic, salt, extra virgin olive oil, chilli oil or chilli sauce, Dijon mustard powder, honey and ground black peppercorns in a bowl. Set aside.

The Salad & Omelette

1 tablespoon miso paste
4 eggs

Whisk the miso paste with the eggs.

1 tablespoon olive oil

Heat olive oil in a non-stick frying pan over medium-high heat.

2 cups chopped button mushrooms

Add mushrooms and sauté until mushrooms are soft.
Add eggs and reduce heat to medium. Let it cook until eggs are set. When the omelette is ready, cut it into strips.

8 big handfuls chopped kale (tough stems discarded)
1/2 teaspoon salt
1/3 cup unsalted chopped raw pecans or walnuts
90 grams grated cheese (preferably Parmesan)

Place the kale in a large bowl and sprinkle salt. Toss kale with some of the dressing, chopped nuts and cheese. Serve with the omelette strips.

RIDGE GOURD

(from left to right)

RIDGE GOURD PRAWN CURRY

RIDGE GOURD PEEL CHUTNEY

Ridge Gourd,
a natural painkiller

Although ridge gourd may be a favourite of many mothers, kids often beg to differ. As they grow into young adults their perspective might change, especially if they find out that it is a perfect cure for a hangover because it has anti-inflammatory properties and is a pain killer too.

Ridge gourd, a member of the cucumber family, has a cooling effect especially in summer. It also helps prevent fungal, viral and bacterial infections and is good for the skin, keeping it clear from pimples and acne. Its high fibre and water content relieves constipation, helps in weight loss, blood purification and also lowers blood sugar levels, thus is excellent for diabetics.

The vegetable can be stir-fried or used in curries. It can also be boiled and added to soups or stews in paste form. The skin is rich in fibre and iron. It is often discarded, but can be used to prepare tangy spiced chutney that can served with dosa or roti wrap, or as a spread on toast or as a dip with cucumber, carrot and celery.

POSITIVE TAKEAWAYS

+ Painkiller
+ Antioxidant and anti-inflammatory
+ Blood purifier

RIDGE GOURD PEEL CHUTNEY

PREPARATION TIME : UNDER 10 MINUTES
SERVES : 4-6

V GF

1 tablespoon oil (preferably sesame oil)
1 teaspoon cumin seeds
1 teaspoon mustard seeds
1 teaspoon coriander seeds
1 sprig curry leaves

---

3 dried red chillies
2 large garlic cloves
1 small onion, chopped
2 cups ridge gourd peel
1/4 cup scraped fresh coconut

1 teaspoon tamarind pulp
A pinch of asafoetida (hing)
Salt to taste

Heat oil in a non-stick pan, add cumin seeds, mustard seeds, coriander seeds and curry leaves and let the seeds splutter.

Add red chillies, garlic and onion and sauté till lightly browned. Add ridge gourd peel and sauté on medium heat till the peels become soft.

Add coconut and sauté for 1 minute, transfer everything onto a plate and let it cool down to room temperature.

Transfer the mixture into a mixer jar, add tamarind pulp, asafoetida and salt and grind into a fine paste. Add 1-2 tablespoons water if required.

Transfer into a bowl and serve as an accompaniment.

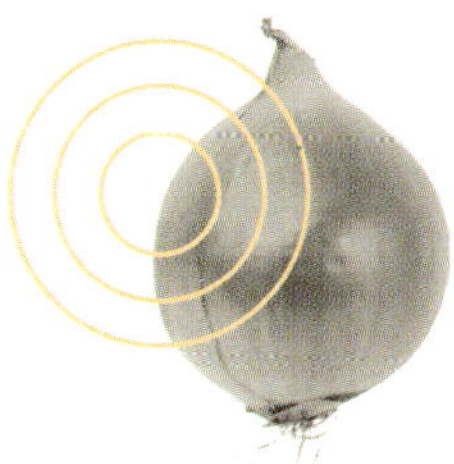

RIDGE GOURD PEEL DOSA

PREPARATION TIME : 1 HOUR OR 5 MINUTES (BY ALTERNATIVE METHOD)
SERVES : 2

V GF

Traditionally 3:1 ratio of rice:dal is taken, soaked for 6 hours and then ground and fermented overnight. That is what we have called in this recipe as ready batter. However, if you have no batter but want dosa immediately, then soak the rice with only 1 tablespoon of dal for an hour, grind and use immediately.

1 cup rice
1 tablespoon split skinless black gram (white urad dal)

1 cup ridge gourd peel
½ bunch fresh coriander leaves
3 sprigs of curry leaves
3 green chillies
1 inch ginger
½ teaspoon cumin seeds
Salt to taste
---
1 medium carrot, grated
1 medium onion, chopped
1 tablespoon oil

To follow the quick method :
Soak the rice and urad dal separately for 1 hour.

In the blender add ridge gourd peel, coriander leaves, curry leaves, green chillies, ginger, cumin seeds, salt, rice, urad dal and blend it into a dosa batter consistency.

Heat the tawa and pour one ladleful of batter, spread the dosa, sprinkle the carrots and onions and cook the dosa using oil.

Alternatively,
Grind the ridge gourd peel, coriander leaves, curry leaves, green chillies, ginger, cumin seeds and salt. Add this to the ready dosa batter. Make dosa by spreading this batter on a hot tawa.

RIDGE GOURD PRAWN CURRY

PREPARATION TIME : 25 MINUTES
SERVES : 4

300 grams ridge gourds
500 grams medium prawns

2 tablespoons oil

2 medium onions
6 garlic cloves
1 inch ginger
1 medium dried red chilli
1/2 teaspoon cumin seeds
1 teaspoon coriander seeds

---

1 teaspoon cumin seeds
1 teaspoon mustard seeds
1 big dried red chilli
1 large onion, finely chopped
4 garlic cloves, finely chopped

---

1 teaspoon turmeric powder
2 teaspoons red chilli powder
Salt to taste

---

1 large tomato, finely chopped
1 teaspoon cumin powder
2 teaspoons coriander powder
1 1/2 teaspoons garam masala powder

---

3 tablespoons chopped fresh coriander leaves

Peel ridge gourds and cut into medium sized roundels. Peel, de-vein and wash prawns thoroughly.

Heat 1 tablespoon oil in a non-stick pan on medium heat. Add prawns and cook. Turn them after 3 minutes and cook for 3 minutes more. Set aside in a bowl.

Grind onions, garlic, ginger, dried red chilli, cumin seeds and coriander seeds with 3 tablespoons of water into a fine paste. Transfer into another bowl and set aside.

Heat 1 tablespoon oil in the same pan. Add cumin seeds, mustard seeds and dried red chilli and let the seeds splutter. Add onion and garlic. Sauté for 2 minutes.

Add the ground paste, turmeric powder, red chilli powder and salt and sauté for 5 minutes.

Add tomato, cumin powder and coriander powder and sauté for 3 minutes.
Add ridge gourd and 1/2 teaspoon garam masala powder and mix well. Cover and cook on medium heat for 5 minutes.

Add prawns, 1 cup water, 2 tablespoons coriander leaves, 1 teaspoon garam masala and mix. Cover and cook for 5 minutes on a low heat.

Transfer into a serving dish, garnish with remaining coriander leaves and serve.

TURMERIC

(from left to right)

CARROT SALAD WITH FRESH TURMERIC

AVOCADO TURMERIC DIP

Turmeric,
the root for weight loss

Although turmeric has recently caught on all over the world as a pill for weight loss, it has in fact been a part of Indian culture for a long time, and it is considered to be auspicious. This yellow coloured root has two main varieties: one which is hard, rich in colour and is used for dyeing and the other is softer, larger and lighter in colour and is used for cooking.

Turmeric is a super food, and it contains curcumin, a substance that has anti-viral, anti-bacterial, anti-fungal, antioxidant, anti-carcinogenic, anti-septic and anti-inflammatory properties. Turmeric also aids recovery after surgery and is herbal remedy for arthritis, anemia, coughs, colds, asthma, sinus and indigestion. It boosts hormones in the brain that increase the growth of new neurons and fight depression and Alzheimer's.

To increase the absorption of curcumin into the bloodstream, it is recommended to consume it with piperine (found in black peppercorns). Coconut oil further enhances the absorption of turmeric powder. Include about 2 teaspoons of turmeric as part of your daily diet.

Turmeric also provides a nutritional balance that supplements cannot duplicate.

POSITIVE TAKEAWAYS

- + Fights cold
- + Anti-tumour
- + Antioxidant, anti-inflammatory & anti-fungal
- + Add pepper and coconut oil for better absorption

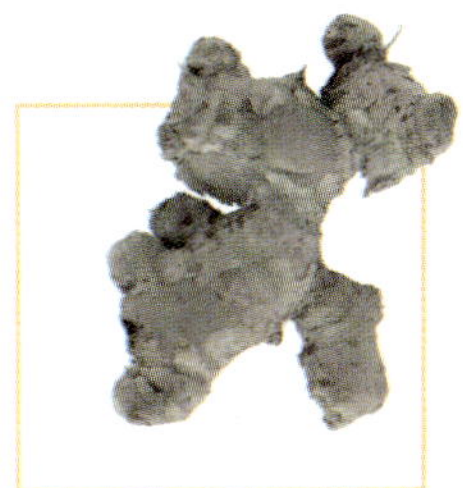

TURMERIC LATTE

PREPARATION TIME : UNDER 10 MINUTES
SERVES : 1

- 100ml coconut milk
- 50ml water
- ½ teaspoon honey
- 1 teaspoon turmeric powder
- ¼ teaspoon black pepper
- ½ teaspoon ginger
- ¼ teaspoon cinnamon powder

Blend all ingredients in a blender until smooth.

Pour into glass and serve chilled.

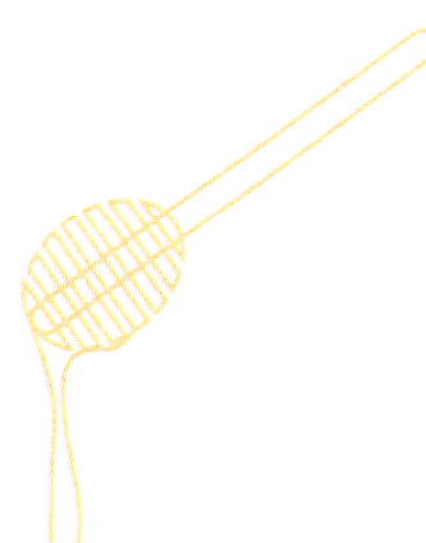

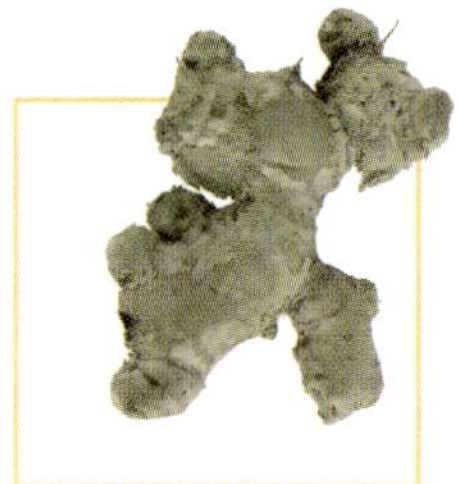

AVOCADO TURMERIC DIP

PREPARATION TIME : 5 MINUTES
SERVES : 2

V GF

- 1/4 avocado, flesh scooped out
- 1 tablespoon turmeric powder
- 4 tablespoons extra virgin olive oil or coconut oil
- 2 lemons (juice & zest)
- 1 garlic clove, minced
- 1 tablespoon honey
- A pinch of salt
- A pinch of black pepper powder

Put avocado, turmeric powder, extra virgin olive oil, lemon juice, lemon zest, garlic, honey, salt and pepper powder in a blender jar and blend.

Add more avocado if you desire a thicker consistency.

Transfer into a bowl and serve.

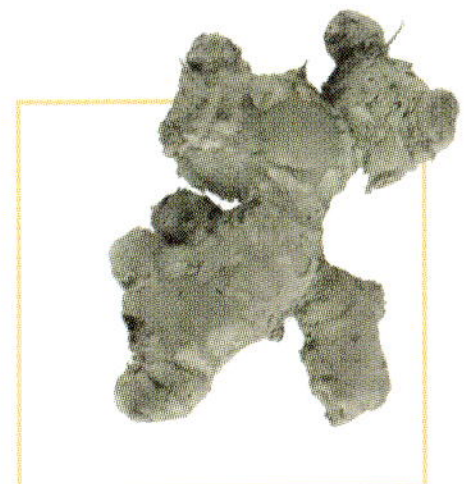

CARROT SALAD WITH FRESH TURMERIC

PREPARATION TIME : UNDER 10 MINUTES
SERVES : 4

V GF

400 grams carrots, finely grated

Take the grated carrots in a salad bowl.

Salt to taste
½ teaspoon black pepper powder
1 two-inch piece fresh turmeric root, finely grated
2 tablespoons coconut oil
3 sprigs of curry leaves, thinly shredded
3 celery stalks, thinly sliced
1 small onion, finely diced
1 medium to large apple, shredded or chopped
2 tablespoons red wine vinegar or balsamic vinegar
2 green chillies, finely chopped

Add salt, pepper powder, fresh turmeric root, oil, curry leaves, celery, onion, apple, vinegar and chillies and mix well. Serve.

ROOT VEGETABLES

(from left to right)

KOKUM MARINATED BEET SALAD

RADISH PINE NUT DIP

Root Vegetables, versatile, wholesome & tasty

A lot of people believe that root vegetables are highly calorific and avoidable. While it is true that root vegetables are carbohydrate rich, they are extremely nutritive and comforting too, especially in colder weather. They are the warmth from underground.

Beets, parsnips, sweet potatoes, turnips and artichokes are root vegetables. They are dense, filling and provide good quality starch. The fibre lowers the glycemic load, causing less digestive or inflammatory problems. In Ayurveda and macrobiotics, it is believed that root vegetables keep us grounded. They are healing and balancing for the body in a state of stress. Root vegetables are also rich in antioxidants, vitamins and minerals. They can be eaten raw or cooked and should be had with the skin.

Turnips are a member of the cruciferous family like broccoli, kale and brussel sprouts. Since they are high in calcium, magnesium and potassium, they are good for the heart.

Radish has antifungal, antibacterial and antioxidant properties. It is rich in minerals, vitamin B and C. It helps relieve constipation and is a remedy for coughs and bronchitis. It is used to treat liver conditions. Radish leaves can be used in a salad or in making pesto. They combine well with nuts and cheese.

Beet is rich in energy and fibre. Since it is rich in nitrate, it is a favorite amongst athletes as it enhances endurance during and post exercise. It is anti-inflammatory, rich in antioxidants, fibre, iron, vitamin C, B6, folate, manganese and potassium. Betanin, the natural pigment which gives beetroot its colour is anti-carcinogenic and builds white blood cells.

Beetroot also helps improve memory and mental alertness because of its high choline content. Choline is a vitamin that helps synthesis of neurotransmitter acetylcholine which helps improve brain memory and is beneficial for Alzheimer sufferers.

Tamarind and kokum are used in most recipes in south India as they combine well with coconut.

Tamarind: The tamarind tree produces pod-like fruit which contains an edible pulp. Tamarind is sweet and sour in taste, and is high in tartaric acid, sugar, vitamin B and calcium. It is high in fibre, vitamin B, potassium, magnesium and iron. The tartaric acid provides a potent antioxidant especially vitamin E. Tamarind works as a laxative.

Kokum is a deep purple fruit that is very similar to mangosteen. It has anti-bacterial and anti-inflammatory properties. It is rich in antioxidants and fibre.

Unlike tamarind, kokum is not acidic. It is a cure for acidity, flatulence and bloating, as it helps maintain a good acid alkaline balance. It is used as a healing herb for ulcers, colds, ear infections, urinary tract infections and rheumatism. It is used to reduce cholesterol and anxiety. It is also a weight loss aid as it controls appetite and optimizes fat burning.

POSITIVE TAKEAWAYS

+ Comforting & wholesome
+ High fibre
+ Rich in antioxidants, vitamins & minerals

KOKUM MARINATED BEET SALAD

PREPARATION TIME : MARINATE FOR 2 HOURS
SERVES : 2
CONTAINS NUTS (OPTIONAL)

1 large beetroot

Dice beet with skin.

2-3 pieces of kokum, mixed with water and made into pulp
Salt to taste

Take beet slices in a bowl, add kokum pulp and salt and mix well. Set aside to marinate for about 2 hours.

Remove beet from marinade and put in a salad bowl. (Use the kokum marinade for a drink or in a dal.)

Radish leaves or any salad greens, as required
Few baby fenugreek leaves or micro greens
Alfalfa sprouts or fenugreek sprouts, as required
1/4 yellow capsicum, diced
2 baby onions, grilled
4 cubes tofu, goat cheese or feta cheese.
Few macadamia nuts or pine nuts

Add radish leaves, baby fenugreek leaves, alfalfa sprouts, yellow capsicum, baby onions, cheese, macadamia nuts or pine nuts and salt and mix well.

Serve immediately.

RADISH PINE NUT DIP

PREPARATION TIME : 5 MINUTES
SERVES : 4

8 medium radishes

1 tablespoon pine nuts + for sprinkling

1 ¹/₄ cups low-fat plain Greek yogurt or hung curd
2 tablespoons mayonnaise
3 tablespoons olive oil
1 teaspoon finely chopped garlic
Few fresh parsley sprigs, finely chopped
2 teaspoons spring onions, finely chopped
Salt to taste
Freshly ground black peppercorns
¹/₄ teaspoon lemon zest

Cucumber wedges (for serving)

Grate the radish and put into a bowl.

Toast pine nuts in a non-stick pan over medium-high heat, tossing often, till golden brown. Transfer into a small bowl and set aside to cool.

Add radish, yogurt, mayonnaise, 2 tablespoons olive oil, garlic, parsley and spring onions and mix well. Season with salt, ground peppercorns and a little lemon zest and mix again.

Sprinkle with pine nuts and remaining lemon zest and drizzle with remaining oil. Serve with cucumber wedges.

SWEET POTATO

(from left to right)

CHICKEN BLACK BEAN STEW
WARM SWEET POTATO & EGG SALAD
ROSEMARY SWEET POTATO WEDGES

Sweet Potato, the fibrous root

Did you know that potato and sweet potato are not from the same family? People with rheumatoid arthritis should avoid potatoes (which belong to the nightshade family) but they can have sweet potatoes (which belongs to the morning glory family).

Even though sweet potato contains 80% water, it is fibrous and filling. Most of the fibre is contained in the skin. It is best had baked with the skin, steamed or simply boiled. It is also rich in vitamin A, vitamin C, B6, E, potassium and iron and is low in sodium. It is a better source of vitamin E than nuts and avocados as it contains virtually no fat.

Sweet potato helps promote digestive health due to its high fibre content, immune functions due to vitamin A and C, fluid and electrolyte balance due to its high potassium content, heart functions especially blood pressure and cholesterol.

Among root vegetables, sweet potato offers the lowest glycemic index rating. Even diabetics can enjoy a sweet potato.

Yam, a commonly used sweet potato, is traditionally used as a medicine to cure piles, arthritis, bronchitis, asthma, coughs and cold. It is also used for long term hormonal balance.

POSITIVE TAKEAWAYS

+ Rich in Vitamin E
+ High in fibre
+ Boiled sweet potato has lower glycemic index than baked sweet potato

CHICKEN BLACK BEAN STEW

PREPARATION TIME : 15-20 MINUTES
SERVES : 4-6

GF

- 1 tablespoon olive oil
- 1 large onion, diced

Heat olive oil in a large non-stick pot on medium heat, add onion and sauté till the onion turns soft.

- 4 cups chicken broth
- 5-6 fire roasted tomatoes, diced
- 1½ cups cooked black beans
- 1 heaped teaspoon smoked paprika
- Salt to taste
- Black pepper powder, to taste

Add chicken broth, tomatoes, beans, smoked paprika, salt, and pepper powder. Mix and bring the mixture to a boil.

- 2 medium sweet potatoes, diced with skin

Reduce heat to low and add sweet potatoes and simmer till sweet potatoes are cooked through.

- 2 cups cooked shredded chicken
- 2 tablespoons chopped fresh parsley

Mash the potato to thicken the stew. Turn the heat off and add chicken and parsley and mix well. Let the stew get heated through.

Serve hot, garnished with parsley.

WARM SWEET POTATO & EGG SALAD

PREPARATION TIME : 10 MINUTES
SERVES : 4

2 large sweet potatoes, boiled with skin	Cut sweet potatoes vertically into thin slices.
	Heat a non-stick grill pan and grill the slices on it for 2 minutes on each side or till grill marks appear on both sides. Remove onto a plate.
1 garlic clove, crushed	Add garlic and grill for 30 seconds.
4 boiled eggs	Peel and quarter the boiled eggs. The yolks should still be a little soft.
130 grams mixed salad leaves 100 grams cherry tomatoes, halved	Arrange the salad leaves and tomatoes equally on 4 plates, top with the sweet potato slices and egg quarters.
1 tablespoon olive oil Juice of ½ lemon Salt to taste	Mix olive oil, lemon juice and salt in a small bowl. Pour this dressing over the salad and serve immediately.

ROSEMARY SWEET POTATO WEDGES

PREPARATION TIME : 20 MINUTES
SERVES : 4 (DIABETICS SHOULD LIMIT QUANTITY)

Preheat oven to 450°F/230°C.

- 2 tablespoons olive oil
- 1 tablespoon chopped fresh rosemary (or 2 teaspoons dried)

Heat olive oil in a small non-stick pan over medium heat. Add rosemary and sauté.

- 3 medium sweet potatoes, scrubbed clean
- 1 teaspoon salt
- ¼ teaspoon freshly ground black peppercorns

Cut sweet potatoes with the skin, lengthwise into 1½ inch thick wedges and place in a large bowl. Add salt and pepper and mix.

Drizzle the rosemary oil over the potatoes and toss gently.

Arrange the wedges on a large baking sheet in one flat layer keeping some distance between each.

Bake in the upper part of the oven, turning the potatoes after 10 minutes. Cook for 20 minutes or till the wedges are soft and lightly browned.

Season again with salt and pepper powder, and remove carefully from the baking sheet. (The wedges are relatively fragile after cooking.)

Serve hot with radish or turmeric dip.

ENERGIZERS

THE 'GO' FOODS

CEREALS

BERRIES, CHIA SEEDS OAT PARFAIT

Carbohydrates, are they really bad for you?

Carbohydrates have earned a bad name for themselves as they can lead to obesity, particularly if too many of them are eaten in one meal. This is because carbohydrates that do not get metabolized get deposited as fat. It is true that one should stay away from a meal high in carbs, especially at night, when less energy is required.

However, carbohydrates are essential in providing energy to meet the body's daily needs. Almost half your diet should comprise of carbohydrates, including cereals, fruits, salads, vegetables and sugar. In the absence of carbohydrates, the body first uses protein for energy, resulting in muscle waste. After that, fat is used for energy, and when fat is broken down, Ketones are released. Besides this, fat takes a longer time to metabolize and uses more oxygen than carbohydrates do.

To slow the rate of absorption of glucose, combine cereals with:

- Protein rich, low glycemic index foods like goat cheese, paneer, curd, peanuts, seeds, etc.
- High fibre green vegetables like fresh fenugreek leaves, spinach.
- Water rich vegetables like bottle gourd (lauki), cabbage etc.

It is important to choose your carbohydrates wisely.

POSITIVE TAKEAWAYS

+ Carbohydrates are essential
+ They provide energy

Cereals,
the energy source

Grains can be legumes or cereals. They are an extremely good source of complex carbohydrates.

Whole grains are low in fat and have no cholesterol; they contain B-vitamins, soluble and insoluble fibre, folate, zinc, protein, iron, magnesium, phytonutrients and antioxidants. In the process of refining, grains lose about 25% of their protein content.

Cereals are of two types - true cereals (grasses) or pseudo-cereals (non-grasses). True cereals may be with gluten and non-gluten cereals. All psuedo cereals are gluten-free.

Gluten containing cereals:
Most of these are high in calcium, phosphorus, manganese, potassium, B-vitamins and selenium.

Wheat: All forms of wheat (bulgur, durum, semolina, spelt, farro, couscous) contain fair amounts of protein and dietary fibre.

Rye: It has a low glycemic index and is high in fibre and antioxidants. It helps in weight loss.

Barley (jau): It is soft, bland, rich in fibre (even more than oats) and vitamin E. It lowers cholesterol, flushes the kidneys and is an excellent cure for urinary infection.

BARLEY RISOTTO

PREPARATION TIME : 10-15 MINUTES
SERVES : 4
(CONTAINS CHEESE; LOW GLYCEMIC INDEX)

270 grams pearl barley, well rinsed	Cook barley in a pressure cooker.
1 tablespoon olive oil 2 garlic cloves, peeled and quartered	Heat olive oil in a non-stick pan over medium heat, add garlic and sauté till golden.
400 grams tomatoes, peeled and chopped 350 grams tomatoes, crushed ½ teaspoon smoked paprika ⅛ teaspoon dried chilli flakes 1 tablespoon fresh thyme ½ teaspoon fresh lemon zest Salt to taste	Add both chopped and crushed tomatoes, paprika, chilli flakes, thyme, lemon zest, salt, barley and a ladleful of water and mix well. Once the mixture comes to a boil, reduce heat and simmer till all the moisture is absorbed.
--- 20 grams chopped fresh coriander leaves or basil leaves Freshly ground black peppercorns 200 grams feta, crumbled roughly	Once done, remove the pan from heat, add coriander leaves or basil leaves, some freshly ground black peppercorns and feta. Mix well and serve hot.

BERRIES, CHIA SEEDS OAT PARFAIT

PREPARATION TIME : 10 MINUTES + REFRIGERATE OVERNIGHT
SERVES : 1 (CONTAINS NUTS)

- 1/2 cup oats
- 1-2 tablespoons cranberries (optional)
- 1 tablespoon chia seeds or flax seeds
- 1 inch ginger, chopped
- 1/2 tablespoon honey
- 1 pinch of cinnamon powder
- 1 tablespoon slivered almonds
- 1 cup yogurt or almond milk or keffir

The evening before you want to serve the oats, take oats in a large bowl, add cranberries, chia seeds, ginger, honey, cinnamon powder and almonds and mix well. Add enough almond milk or yogurt or keffir so that all the ingredients soak thoroughly for about 15 minutes.

Add some more almond milk or yogurt as the oats will have soaked up a lot of moisture and also the chia seeds and cranberries will have started to gel up.
(You can add almond milk to the yogurt to get the right consistency or dilute thick yogurt with water, so that the oats can soak thoroughly)

- 1 handful chopped walnuts
- 1 handful blueberries or grapes
- 1/2 ripe banana, sliced into roundels
- 1/3 cup chopped pineapple or any seasonal fruit
- 1 tablespoon granola

Keep this mixture in the refrigerator overnight. In the morning before serving, add walnuts, blueberries, banana and pineapple or any fruit of your choice. Top it with granola for the crunch.

CEREALS

(from left to right)

SAGO/SABUDANA WAFFLES

BUCKWHEAT CRÊPES

Pseudo-cereals, the energy source

Most people, especially youngsters are unaware of alternative cereals. Others use them only as foods to be eaten during religious fasts, oblivious of their benefits.

Pseudo-cereals:
They resemble cereals but are made from fruits and seeds. In India these are used in place of cereals during religious fasts and are healthy enough to incorporate in everyday cooking. These foods are all gluten-free, easily digestible, cleansing and detoxifying. Most are fairly rich in protein, minerals and fibre. They are rich in iron, magnesium, phosphorus and manganese. However, some of them are starchy, and high in calories.

Buckwheat (kuttu): It is a seed of a plant related to rhubarb and has a rich, nutty flavour. It is the only grain known to have high levels of an antioxidant called rutin. It is high in essential fatty acids and soluble fibre and has a low glycemic index.

Water chestnut flour (singhare ka atta): It has a low glycemic index, low calorific value, high vitamin content and high fibre content. It is free from cholesterol and fat, and has great detoxifying and cooling properties.

Arrowroot powder is extracted from various tropical tubers and is used to thicken curries. It is the most digestible of all flours. It maintains acid alkaline balance and aids digestion. Replace all cornflour recipes with arrowroot for greater health benefits.

Tapioca/sabudana/sago: Starch extracted from a plant, sabudana is extremely low in fat and protein, and has no minerals or vitamins. 100 grams of dry sago would give you 355 calories, including an average of 94 grams of carbohydrate. It is great for weight gain.

Banana flour is the highest form of resistant starch, a prebiotic which promotes the growth of good bacteria in the gut and can also assist with weight loss.

Coconut flour is high in fibre, protein and healthy fats. It is also low in carbohydrates and calories. It has a low glycemic index.

Amaranth & quinoa are also pseudo-cereals which have been covered in greater detail in the book.

Note:
- Soaking also applies to all grains (rice, quinoa, barley, burghul, buck-wheat and oats).
- Soaking helps to break down toxins and anti-nutrients like phytic acid.
- Oats contain the highest amount of phytic acid among all grains.
- These phytates block mineral absorption in the gut and can cause gastric distress or bloating in sensitive individuals.
- Soaking also reduces the acidity (makes it alkaline).
- It adds the enzymatic force and begins the sprouting process.

POSITIVE TAKEAWAYS

+ Rich source of vitamins & minerals

SAGO/SABUDANA WAFFLE

PREPARATION TIME : 15 MINUTES
SERVES : 2 (CONTAINS NUTS)
HIGH CARBOHYDRATE & HIGH GLYCEMIC INDEX

2 medium potatoes, boiled with skin
1 whole egg or 3 egg whites (optional)
1/2 cup sago/sabudana, soaked overnight

1/4 cup coarsely powdered, peanuts
Salt to taste
Black pepper powder to taste
2 teaspoons cumin powder
1 teaspoon chaat masala
1 green chilli, chopped finely
1 tablespoon chopped fresh coriander leaves
Juice of 1/2 lemon

Put potatoes in a bowl and mash them well with their skin. Add egg (or egg whites) and sago and beat well together.

Add peanuts, salt, pepper powder, cumin powder, chaat masala, green chilli, coriander leaves and lemon juice and mix together till well blended.

Heat a waffle iron. Pour a little mixture into it and cook till done. Make more waffles with the remaining batter.

Serve the waffles with green chutney.

Note:
This is a favourite for all ages from the young to the old. I often add egg to this recipe to complete the protein. It also brings down the glycemic index. It is traditionally had as Aloo Sabudana Khichdi.

BUCKWHEAT CRÊPES

PREPARATION TIME : UNDER 10 MINUTES
MAKES : 10 (6" CRÊPES)

70 grams (3/4 cup) buckwheat flour (kuttu ka atta)
Salt to taste
1 1/2 cups unsweetened almond milk
3 large eggs (optional)

---

1 tablespoon olive oil
1 medium onion, diced
1 garlic clove, minced
1 small broccoli, small florets separated
200 grams mushrooms, cleaned and chopped coarsely
1 teaspoon dried thyme
Salt to taste
Black pepper powder to taste
2 cups stemmed & chopped kale
(Any green leaves like spinach or amaranth can replace kale)

To make crêpes blend together buckwheat flour, salt, almond milk, and eggs. Transfer into a bowl. Set aside.

To make stuffing, heat oil in another non-stick pan. Add onion, garlic, broccoli, mushrooms, thyme, salt and pepper powder and stir-fry for 2-3 minutes. Add kale or any green leaf and cook for 1 minute more. Set aside to cool.

Heat a non-stick pan and grease it lightly. Pour 2 serving spoons batter into the pan, swirl to spread the batter evenly all around the pan. Cook till bubbles appear and the crêpe is set. Carefully flip the crêpe and cook the other side too. Transfer onto a plate. Similarly make more pancakes.

Put a little filling in the centre of each crêpe, roll and serve immediately.

Note:
You can also apply avocado, cream, cheese spread or salsa or mayonnaise on the crêpe before stuffing them.

AMARANTH

(from left to right)

AMARANTH CRUSTED CHICKEN

AMARANTH OMELETTE

Amaranth (Rajgira), God's grain

In India, Rajgira is traditionally eaten while fasting during festivals, especially during Navratri. Whereas in Mexico, it is sold as a super health food. It is high in protein, and has anti-inflammatory as well as cholesterol and blood pressure lowering properties. Amaranth compares very closely to quinoa. It is as high in its protein content as quinoa.

Its grain is very light in colour and weight, and has a high glycemic index. It is high in fibre and has more calcium than most other grains.

It is high in lysine, an amino acid found in few foods. It is also rich in minerals like iron, manganese and phosphorus. Amaranth leaves are a good source of vitamin A, B, C, folate and minerals. It is a super food ideal for diabetic or celiac intolerant people because of its low glycemic index value and absence of gluten.

Amaranth is extremely versatile, and can be consumed in a variety of ways. It can be used to replace rice, pasta or couscous. It can also be used to make upma, idlis, rotis, crêpes, pancakes, waffles or muffins. It is a good alternative to quinoa, and can be used in porridge, kheer, kadhi or chikki.

POSITIVE TAKEAWAYS

+ Superfood that is high in protein
+ Versatile; both its grains and leaves can be used

Quinoa, the protein-rich cereal

Quinoa, a seed of a beet relative, belongs to the amaranth family. It has the perfect balance of all nine amino acids essential for our well-being. This type of complete protein is rarely found in plant foods, though it is commonly found in meats.

Quinoa is therefore an excellent choice for vegans who may struggle to get enough protein in their diets. This gluten-free grain is among the least allergenic grains. Both its grains and leaves are edible.

It is also anti-inflammatory and high in antioxidants, fibre, iron, several B-vitamins and vitamin E. It is very high in minerals like calcium. It has phytates and oxalates that prevent absorption of minerals. Fortunately, the impact of these inhibitors can be reduced by soaking or sprouting.

Although it has a low glycemic index, it is high in carbohydrates and rich in monounsaturated fats. There are 111 calories in each 1/2 cup of cooked quinoa.

Quinoa is covered with saponin, which gives it a bitter taste and can be removed by thorough rinsing. Always soak the quinoa and rinse thoroughly before cooking. Cooked quinoa seeds become fluffy and creamy, yet maintain a slight crunch. They have a delicate and subtly nutty flavour. Use it as a breakfast cereal, in pancakes, fritters, salad, upma, khichdi, puddings, smoothies, or as quinoa milk.

POSITIVE TAKEAWAYS

+ Quinoa has 9 essential proteins
+ High in fibre, antioxidants & minerals
+ Gluten-free cereal with a low glycemic index

AMARANTH OMELETTE

PREPARATION TIME : 10 MINUTES
SERVES : 4

GF

6 eggs
Salt to taste
Black pepper powder to taste
---
1 tablespoon oil
3 garlic cloves, chopped
---
225 grams amaranth leaves, stemmed

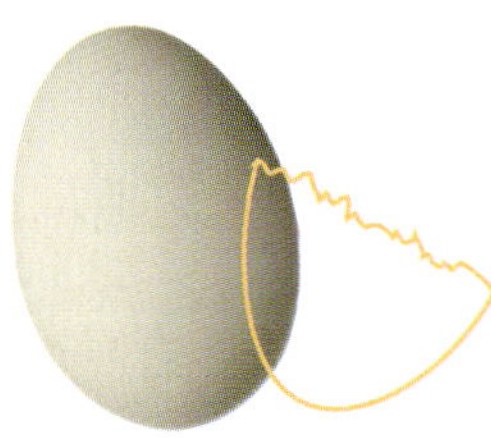

Break the eggs into a bowl, add salt and pepper powder and whisk well.

Heat oil in a small non-stick pan on high heat, add garlic and sauté till fragrant.

Add amaranth, mix and cook covered till the leaves start to wilt.

Spread out the leaves evenly on the pan.

Pour the eggs over the amaranth. Turn the heat down to medium and cook the egg mixture for about 2 minutes or till partially set. Tilt the pan to the side and use spatula to partially lift that side of the omelette to allow the runny part to run underneath. Do this to the other sides if needed.

Continue cooking till the eggs are completely cooked.
Cut into wedges and serve hot.

AMARANTH CRUSTED CHICKEN

PREPARATION TIME : 20-30 MINUTES
SERVES : 2

GF

680 grams boneless, skinless chicken breasts

Preheat oven to 400°F/200°C.
Cut chicken into 6 pieces. Flatten them with a steak hammer to 1/2 inch thickness and put into a bowl.

Juice of 1 lemon
4 teaspoons olive oil
1 tablespoon Dijon mustard
2 teaspoons fresh garlic, minced

To make the marinade, whisk together lemon juice, olive oil, Dijon mustard and garlic well. Add the mixture to the chicken and mix well so that the all the pieces are well covered. Set aside to marinate for 10 minutes.

6 tablespoons amaranth seeds

Heat a non-stick pan over high heat till it becomes very hot. Add amaranth seeds and cover with a lid. Shake the pan until all the seeds have popped. Remove seeds from the pan and spread on a plate.

3 teaspoons olive oil
6 mini capsicums (red, orange, yellow) or bhavnagri mirch
Pinch of sea salt
Pinch of black pepper powder

To make roasted capsicums, grease a baking tray with oil. Place capsicums on it and drizzle some oil over them. Sprinkle salt and pepper powder. Place the tray in the preheated oven and bake for 10 minutes. To brown evenly, turn capsicums and bake for 10 minutes more.

Heat olive oil in a non-stick pan, place the chicken in it and sauté, turning sides, till light golden on both sides. Cover with a lid, lower heat and cook till the chicken is done.

Place the chicken pieces over the roasted amaranth seeds and coat both sides evenly.

Serve the chicken hot with roasted capsicums.

CEREALS

(from left to right)
BUCKWHEAT
QUINOA
DALIA
OATS
SOBA NOODLES

QUINOA PIZZA

PREPARATION TIME : 20 MINUTES
SERVES : 2 (MAKES 1 9-INCH PIZZA BASE)

Preheat the oven to 425°F/220°C.

3/4 cup quinoa

Take quinoa in a small bowl and cover it with water and let it soak for 1 hour. Drain and rinse thoroughly. (This will prevent any bitterness in the crust.)

1 teaspoon baking powder
Salt to taste

Put the quinoa, sufficient water, baking powder and salt in a food processor. Process till a smooth batter is formed.

Line a round cake pan with parchment paper and spray the parchment paper with cooking spray.

Parchment paper can be replaced by foil or just greasing the dish and then dusting it with flour.

Pour the batter into the pan, place the pan in the preheated oven and bake for 15 minutes.

Flip the crust over and bake for 5-10 minutes more, till golden and the edges are crisp. Remove from the oven.

Tomato paste or hummus
A few thin strips of green, red and yellow capsicums
Grated mozzarella cheese, as required (optional)

Top with tomato paste or hummus, capsicums and cheese. Cut into wedges and serve warm. Cook for 5 minutes to melt cheese.

QUINOA CHICKPEAS SALAD

PREPARATION TIME : 5-10 MINUTES
SERVES : 2 (CONTAINS CHEESE & NUTS)

$^{1}/_{3}$ cup chickpeas, soaked overnight

Cook the chickpeas in 1 cup water in a pressure cooker. Drain and put into a mixing bowl. Use the water in any other gravy. do not discard , it is nutrient rich.

1 cup quinoa, soaked for 1 hour and rinsed well

Cook quinoa in 2 cups hot water. Put into the same bowl.

2 tablespoons olive oil
2 teaspoons rice vinegar or red wine vinegar
1 teaspoon honey
$^{1}/_{4}$ teaspoon curry powder

To make the dressing:
Mix together olive oil, rice vinegar, honey and curry powder in a small bowl.

A big handful of flat-leaf parsley, chopped
$^{1}/_{2}$ cup crumbled feta
1 medium apple, chopped

Add parsley, feta and apple to the quinoa mixture and mix well.

$^{1}/_{4}$ cup golden raisins
$^{1}/_{2}$ cup toasted walnuts or almonds or pine nuts

Drizzle dressing over the salad. Sprinkle raisins, toasted walnuts or almonds just before serving.

Optional:
pomegranate, cherry tomatoes, courgette, spring onions

SUGAR

CHOCOLATE COCONUT BALLS

Sugar, an addiction

At its most basic level, sugar is a simple carbohydrate which supplies the body quickly with glucose, which is a source of fuel and energy. In some form or other, it can be found in almost everything we consume.

Traditionally, one thinks of sugar as white crystals of table sugar. However, it is also found as brown sugar, unrefined sugar, gur/jaggery, raw sugar, sugar cane, beet sugar, corn sugar, fruits (as fructose), sucrose, glucose, dextrose, maltose, honey, agave and maple syrup.

Sugar is also prevalent in many hidden forms in breakfast cereals and mentioned on packaging labels as evaporated cane juice, concentrated fruit juice, corn syrup, potato starch, concentrates of orange juice, grape juice or apple juice, molasses and high fructose corn syrup (HFCS).

HFCS is linked to diabetes and obesity. Added sugars - from any source, natural or artificial, add up weight and all have equal adverse effects metabolically.

Sweeteners : They are not absorbed by the body and only satisfy the craving for sugar. The most common ingredients used in sweeteners are saccharin, aspartame and sucralose. Aspartame can be avoided as it contains phenylalanine, an amino acid involved with metabolism.

Stevia is a natural sugar made from a plant. It does not cause insulin levels to spike dramatically. Nevertheless, use it sparingly.

You can replace sugar with natural sweetening ingredients like dried fruits, apple or banana purée or blackstrap molasses. Honey and maple sugar are also very good substitutes of sugar but one can never be certain about their purity.

POSITIVE TAKEAWAYS

+ Sugar gives energy
+ Excess sugar of any kind has negative metabolic impact
+ Read labels for disguised sugar

CHOCOLATE COCONUT BALLS

PREPARATION TIME : UNDER 5 MINUTES
MAKES 10 BALLS (CONTAINS NUTS)

V

1 cup ground walnuts + almonds

Coarsely powder walnuts and almonds in a food processor and transfer into a bowl.

1/2 cup dates

Remove the seeds of the dates and chop into small pieces. Add to the nuts in the bowl and mix.

1-2 tablespoons unsweetened cocoa powder
2 tablespoons desiccated coconut powder
1 tablespoon coconut oil* (optional)

Put cocoa powder, coconut powder and coconut oil in the processor and process till well mixed.

Add this to the bowl with nuts and dates and mix everything well. Divide the mixture into equal portions and roll them into balls. Serve.

**The coconut oil is not crucial to the recipe. Do not substitute it with any other oil.*

GLYCEMIC INDEX

(from left to right)

BROCCOLI QUINOA CASSEROLE

STUFFED ZUCCHINI ROLLS

CAULIFLOWER RICE

Glycemic Index, a useful indicator

Glycemic index (GI) tells us how fast and how much a particular food raises blood glucose levels, which when uncontrolled can play havoc with your health. Foods with higher glycemic index are digested rapidly and raise blood sugar levels faster than foods with lower glycemic index, which are digested slowly. A food with a glycemic index of 28 boosts blood sugar only 28% as much as pure glucose which is 100%. A food's GI depends on its fibre content, cooking and processing method, and on the combinations of various foods in a meal. Only carbohydrates release sugar when they are broken down, and traditional carbs like potatoes and white rice are high GI foods. On the other hand, dals, lentils, pulses and dairy products are low GI foods as they are primarily proteins but also have some carbohydrates.

Choose low glycemic index foods to control diabetes, weight and cholesterol. Add protein (e.g. nuts), fats (e.g. avocado) and fibre (e.g. flax seeds) to a meal to keep your GI in check.

Try: Ussal pav, idli sambhar, ragda pattice, chole rice, rajma rice, khichdi, paneer paratha with curd, pasta with fish, noodles with tofu.

POSITIVE TAKEAWAYS

+ It measures the increase in blood glucose levels
+ Rapidly digested foods have a high index
+ Balance high glycemic index foods with protein & fibre

HIGH > 70	MEDIUM 56-59	LOW 1-55*
Potatoes	Sweet corn	Green vegetables
White Rice	Banana	Nuts
White bread	Pineapple	Papaya
Bagels	Raisins	Apple
Cornflakes	Oats	Guava
Biscuits	(breakfast cereals)	Raw carrots
Cookies	Multigrain	Mushrooms
Cupcakes	Oat bran	Broccoli
Cereals	Rye bread	Cabbage
		Capsicums
		Kidney beans
		Chickpeas
		Lentils
		Bran
		Peas
		Quinoa
		Barley
		Par boiled rice
		(black or brown)

*Contains high fibre

BROCCOLI QUINOA CASSEROLE

PREPARATION TIME : 30 MINUTES
SERVES : 5 (CONTAINS CHEESE)

GF

3/4 cups broccoli florets	Preheat oven to 400°F/200°C. Spread broccoli florets on a greased tray, place the tray in the preheated oven and roast for 5 minutes.
1 cup vegetable stock 1 tablespoon pesto Salt to taste Crushed black peppercorns to taste	In a large mixing bowl, mix the vegetable stock, pesto, salt and peppercorns. Heat mixture until it boils.
--- 1 1/2 cups uncooked quinoa 1 spring onion, chopped 1 cup shredded spinach 3 tablespoons Parmesan cheese 200 grams mozzarella cheese	Take quinoa and spring onions in a casserole. Add vegetable stock mixture, spinach, Parmesan and 3/4 of the mozzarella cheese. Place the tray in the preheated oven and bake for 30 minutes.
	Take the casserole out of the oven and add broccoli. Sprinkle remaining mozzarella cheese on top, place the casserole back in the oven and bake till the cheese melts.
Red chilli flakes to taste	Sprinkle red chilli flakes and serve.

STUFFED ZUCCHINI ROLLS

PREPARATION TIME : UNDER 5 MINUTES
MAKES 15-20 ROLLS
(CONTAINS CHEESE & NUTS)

4 small zucchini, ends trimmed (use cucumber or courgette if zucchini is not available)

Olive oil as required
3-4 tablespoons balsamic vinegar & to sprinkle

Slice each zucchini lengthways into 6 thin long strips.

Drizzle some olive oil over 2 large trays. Place the zucchini slices flat on the trays. Do not overlap. Sprinkle some oil and balsamic vinegar over the slices. Cover and leave to marinate for 10 minutes in the refrigerator.

50 grams pine nuts

Roast the pine nuts in a non-stick pan till lightly browned. Transfer into a bowl.

250 grams ricotta cheese
Handful fresh basil leaves, chopped
Juice of ½ lemon

Add ricotta cheese, basil, lemon juice and olive oil and mix.

Place 1 teaspoon of ricotta cheese mixture on one end of each zucchini strip and roll up. The filling will hold the zucchini roll together. There is no need to secure with a toothpick.

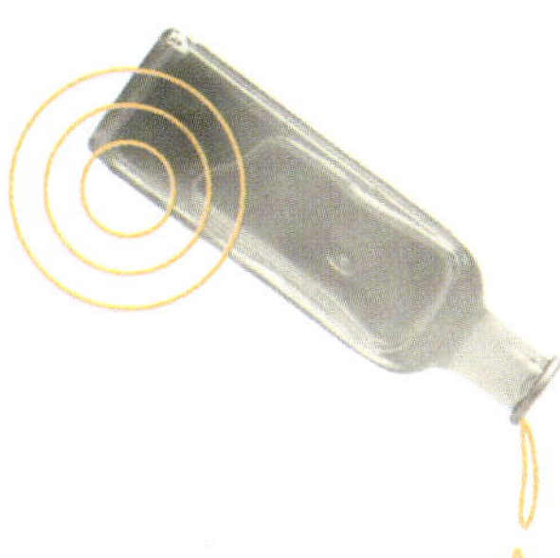

Arrange rolls upright on a plate and sprinkle some freshly ground black peppercorns, olive oil and balsamic vinegar.

Serve immediately.

CAULIFLOWER RICE

PREPARATION TIME : UNDER 10 MINUTES
SERVES : 4
(LOW CARBOHYDRATE)

1 tablespoons oil 3 garlic cloves, minced	Heat oil in a non-stick pan, add garlic and sauté till garlic flavour is infused into the oil. Take care that the garlic does not burn.
1 medium cauliflower	Mince the cauliflower florets in the blender till they resemble grains of rice or, grate the florets.
3 tablespoons shredded Parmesan or cheddar cheese 1 egg, scrambled (optional) Salt to taste Black pepper powder to taste	Add cauliflower to the pan with garlic and sauté. Add cheese, scrambled egg, salt and pepper powder and continue to sauté till cauliflower is tender. *(Lactose intolerant can omit the cheese or replace it with tofu.)*
A few fresh parsley sprigs, chopped	Serve warm garnished with parsley.

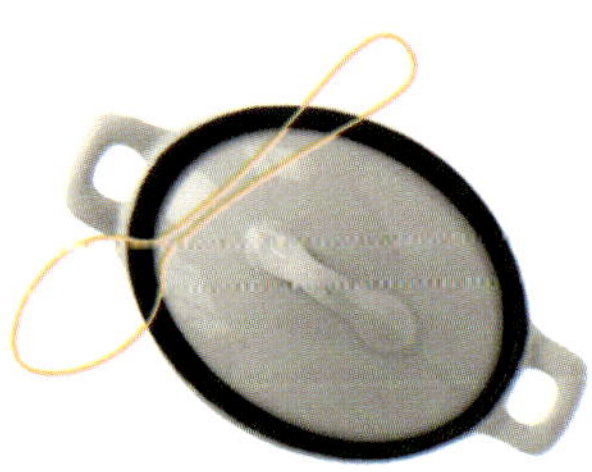

CAULIFLOWER CHICKEN FRIED RICE

PREPARATION TIME : 10 MINUTES
SERVES : 4

GF

2 tablespoons + 1 teaspoon peanut oil
2 large eggs, beaten

Heat 1 teaspoon peanut oil in a non-stick pan. Add eggs and cook, without stirring, till fully cooked on one side. Flip the omelette and cook the other side for about 15 seconds.

Take the omelette off the pan and place on the work top. Cut into 1/2 inch pieces. Keep aside in a plate.

3 spring onion bulbs, thinly sliced
1 tablespoon grated fresh ginger
1 tablespoon minced garlic

Add 1 tablespoon peanut oil to the same pan, add spring onion bulbs, ginger and garlic and sauté, stirring, till the onions soften.

450 grams boneless, skinless chicken thighs, trimmed and cut into 1/2 inch pieces
1/2 cup diced red capsicum
1 cup snow peas, trimmed and halved

Add chicken and cook, stirring, till chicken is almost done.

Add capsicum and snow peas, mix and cook, stirring, till just tender. Transfer onto a large plate.

4 cups cauliflower rice (as mentioned in previous recipe)
3 tablespoons soy sauce
1 teaspoon sesame oil (optional)

Add the remaining 1 tablespoon peanut oil to the same pan. Add cauliflower rice and stir for 2 minutes. Add the chicken mixture and the eggs. Add soy sauce and sesame oil and mix gently till well combined.

3 stalks spring onion greens, thinly sliced

Garnish with spring onion greens and serve hot.

COMMON CONCERNS

TACKLING YOUR EVERYDAY ISSUES

CONSTIPATION
BEET & SPINACH JUICE

Constipation,
painful with no easy solution

For many years I suffered from constipation. I realized that I am not alone and that there is no one solution for all.

Constipation causes a delay in cleansing your system, resulting in unhealthy bacteria and toxins getting accumulated. It can cause headaches, foul breath, bloating of the stomach and flatulence. Acidity also causes constipation and at the same time, constipation can cause acidity.

Causes:
- Medicines containing calcium or aluminum, iron
- Stress
- Lack of fibre, water, sleep, exercise and movement
- Sugar and refined starchy foods
- Packaged foods, additives, preservatives, colourings

Fibre is one of the best cures. It is found in peels, skin, stems, outer leaves of vegetables and fruits. It is important to drink water as fibre absorbs water. Besides, water softens stools.

Please note that too much fibre can reduce absorption of iron and calcium and zinc.

POSITIVE TAKEAWAYS

+ Constipation accumulates toxins and causes acidity
+ Fibre and water are the best cure

Other remedies:

- Water
- Unstrained soup or warm liquid in the morning
- Psyllium husk dietary supplement with plenty of water (Isabgol, Triphala)
- Senna leaves
- Raw green vegetables as juice or salad
- Fruits and dry fruits – guava, orange, papaya, dates, figs, prunes
- Flax seeds, soaked and sprouted fenugreek seeds
- Whole grains and pulses especially oats, popcorn, sprouts, bran
- Ghee, castor oil
- Herbal teas, digestive teas, laxative teas

SPROUTED FENUGREEK & MIXED LENTIL SALAD

PREPARATION TIME : 5 MINUTES
SERVES : 2-4

1 teaspoon ghee or sesame oil
2 dried red chillies, cut into small pieces
2 tablespoons finely chopped ginger
$^{1}/_{4}$ cup chopped curry leaves
Salt to taste

$^{1}/_{4}$ cup mixed lentil sprouts
$^{3}/_{4}$ cup fenugreek sprouts
$^{1}/_{3}$ cup scraped fresh coconut

Black pepper powder to taste
Juice of $^{1}/_{2}$ lemon
1 teaspoon honey

Heat oil in a non-stick pan. Add red chillies, ginger and curry leaves and sauté. Add salt and sauté, stirring, till the mixture is fragrant.

Add mixed lentil sprouts and toss well. Add fenugreek sprouts and coconut and toss everything together. Take the pan off the heat. The sprouts just need to get warm, not to be cooked.

Season with salt, pepper powder, lemon juice and honey and serve.

To sprout:
Soak fenugreek seeds and lentils separately for about 6 hours. Wash and drain off the water. Cover with lid and keep in a warm place for about 24 hours or till they sprouts. Alternatively, tie pre-soaked seeds or lentil in a muslin cloth and keep in a warm place for 24 hours. The sprouts will keep well if refrigerated for 3-4 days.

BEET & SPINACH JUICE

PREPARATION TIME : 5 MINUTES
SERVES : 2-4

2 medium green apples, roughly chopped
3 medium beets, peeled and roughly chopped
2 medium carrots, peeled and roughly chopped
1 cup spinach, roughly chopped
1 teaspoon chia / flax seeds

Put apples, beets, carrots, spinach and flax seeds in a slow/cold press juicer and process.
Note: Avoid high speed mixers/ blenders. Invest in a slow press for a more nutritious juice.

Collect the juice in a jar and pour into individual glasses. Serve.

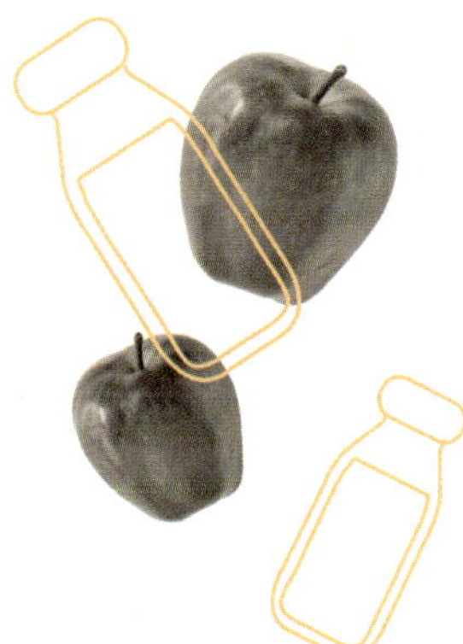

TOXIC INFLAMMATION

(from left to right)

LEAFY VEGGIE WRAP

THE NUTTY WRAP

Toxic Inflammation,
a protective reaction

One typically associates inflammation with physical injury, however inflammation can also be caused by eating certain foods. Inflammation is a response by immune cells to protect the body against bacteria, infection, toxins and invasion by a foreign body.

Additives, preservatives, chemicals, allergens, medicines and junk foods generate toxins which cause inflammation, swelling, bloating and fluid accumulation. Long term inflammation results in lowered immunity, fluctuations in blood sugar levels and irregular sleep patterns. It also leads to blocked arteries, abnormal cell growth which can lead to cancer and tissue destruction resulting in hives, hay fever and rash. It can also lead to hormonal imbalance, autoimmune disease and weight gain.

While omega 3 fats are anti-inflammatory, omega 6 fats cause inflammation. Stay away from corn if you are feeling bloated, as it is high in omega 6. Get out and get in some sunshine, as vitamin D, available from sunlight, is an effective way to stop inflammation.

To find out if you have inflammation, take a test to measure your C-reactive protein or CRP levels. Also take an allergy test to find out which allergens might be causing your inflammation.

POSITIVE TAKEAWAYS

+ Omega 3 fats are anti-inflammatory
+ Long term inflammation lowers immunity

High anti-inflammatory foods include:

- Colourful fruits and vegetables
- Omega 3 fats as present in fish, walnuts, flax seeds
- Almonds and peanut butter
- Herbs and spices: turmeric, ginger, aloe vera, basil and cinnamon
- Garlic, onions, pepper and pineapple

LEAFY VEGGIE WRAP

PREPARATION TIME : 5-10 MINUTES
SERVES : 1-2

V GF

$\frac{1}{4}$ avocado or mayonnaise or hung curd or cream cheese

Scoop out the avocado flesh and put into a small bowl. Use mayonnaise or hung curd or cream cheese, if avocado is not available.

Juice of 1 small lemon
A pinch of cumin powder
A pinch of coriander powder
A pinch of cayenne pepper powder or red chilli powder
1 teaspoon spirulina powder

Mix together most of the lemon juice, cumin powder, coriander powder, cayenne pepper powder and spirulina powder. Mash the avocado and spice together with a fork.

---

1 large collard leaf or romaine lettuce leaves or salad leaves
1 small carrot, peeled and grated
1 tablespoon hemp seeds (optional) or flaxseeds or sesame
Salt to taste
Black pepper powder to taste
1 teaspoon olive oil

Place the leaf on a plate and place the fillings vertically along one long side of the leaf, leaving a margin on each side, in the following order: avocado mixture, carrot, hemp or flaxseed seeds, salt and pepper powder. Drizzle olive oil and the remaining lemon juice.

Roll the salad leaf with filling into a wrap. Serve immediately.

THE NUTTY WRAP

PREPARATION TIME : 5-10 MINUTES
MAKES : 5-6 WRAPS

V GF

2 cups walnuts	Process walnuts in a food processor till coarsely ground and transfer into a bowl.
1 tablespoon cumin powder $1\frac{1}{2}$ teaspoons red chilli powder $1\frac{1}{2}$ teaspoons coriander powder Black pepper to taste 2 tablespoons soy sauce	Add cumin powder, chilli powder, coriander powder and pepper powder and mix. Add soy sauce, mix and set aside.
80 grams quinoa, cooked (optional)	To make it more wholesome, add quinoa to the above mixture and mix well.
6 large collard green leaves, stems removed (can substitute with iceberg lettuce, spinach or pakchoy) 5-6 tablespoons salsa (mix of tomato and onion), as required	Place each trimmed leaf on the work top, dark side facing down. Place $\frac{1}{4}$ to $\frac{1}{2}$ cup walnut mixture, on one side of the leaf. Top mixture with 1 tablespoon salsa. Roll to make a wrap. For additional filling, roll once, add more filling, roll again. Serve with additional salsa.

ACIDITY

(from left to right)

SOBA IN TAHINI SAUCE

SPIRULINA SMOOTHIE

Acidity, a burning issue

Acidity is caused by excess production of acid by the gastric glands of the stomach. It causes gastric inflammation, belching, indigestion and constipation. Constant acidity may result in ulcers.

Hyperacidity is the excess secretion of HCL (hydrochloric acid) in the stomach. It causes a burning sensation, stomach cramps, nausea and a bitter taste in the mouth.

Heartburn is the fiery sensation that grabs hold of your lower chest after eating. Stomach acids reflux into the oesophagus, leaving a sour taste in the mouth and throat.

Acidity is caused because of the following:
- Large gaps between meals
- Eating large meals at a time, especially high in fat
- Spicy foods and pickles
- Drinking insufficient water
- Food allergies

Consume your last meal at least two hours before sleeping.

It's not a good idea to pop in too many antacids as they inhibit absorption of vitamin B12, D, calcium and magnesium.

All foods can be classified as acidic or alkaline. Just because a particular food is acid forming does not mean that you should completely eliminate it from your diet or avoid it for an extended period of time. 80% of alkaline foods and 20% of acid foods provide a good balance of nutrients. Try and eat more alkaline foods to balance acidity.

When acidic, avoid:	**To cure acidity, have:**
Garlic, onion or radish Pepper Coffee Citrus fruits & unripe fruits	Water & electrolytes Chilled milk/coconut water Rice gruel or congee Banana, apple or watermelon

Balance acidic foods (20%):	**With alkaline foods (80%):**
All nuts except almonds All cereals All beans except soy bean All dairy products Eggs All flesh foods Cranberries Vinegar	Chia seeds Quinoa, buckwheat, millets Sprouted legumes Whey, yogurt, almond milk Tofu All vegetables All fruits (except plums and prunes)

Acidity & Muscle Loss,
unneccesary damage

The blood will always take measures to ensure that a neutral blood pH (7) is maintained. When the pH level is acidic, the body must neutralize the excess dietary acids. The two main ways the body does this is by taking calcium (and other minerals) from bones and glutamine (a protein) from the skeletal muscle and this can lead to muscle protein loss.

Besides, as we age, there is a natural loss of muscle mass and gradual changes in the kidney functions. This tends leaves the body in an acidic state.

High acid levels can cause a drop in bone density, bone mineral levels and muscle mass. Lactic acid released during a workout does not increase blood acid levels, because the body uses lactic acid as fuel during the exercise. However, when more lactic acid is produced than used, the muscle may cramp, become sore, or even reach a point of failure. At this stage the body is acidic.

Positive acid/alkaline balance is one of the most important factors in athletic performance. Furthermore, athletes require more food in general with an emphasis on protein to aid muscle recovery.

The paradox is this: most protein sources are highly acid forming and the highly alkaline forming foods are generally low in protein.

Sprouted legumes, lentils, beans, tofu, yogurt, sesame, flax seeds, hemp are superior sources of alkalizing protein. Fibre has the ability to help maintain muscle and bone.

POSITIVE TAKEAWAYS

+ Acids break down muscle
+ Acidity reduces calcium and lower bone density
+ Maintain an 80:20 alkaline:acid ratio

RATATOUILLE SHEPHERD'S PIE

PREPARATION TIME : 20 MINUTES
SERVES : 6

V GF

Preheat oven to 375°F/190°C. Grease a large, deep pie pan or medium-sized casserole.

- 1½ tablespoons olive oil
- 1½ cups chopped onion

Heat olive oil in large non-stick pan over medium heat, add onion and sauté, stirring often, for 5 minutes.

- 1 medium eggplant, diced
- 2 cups diced zucchini

Add eggplant and zucchini, cover partially and cook, stirring often, for 3-4 minutes.

- 1 cup sliced button mushrooms
- 1 cup green peas
- 2 teaspoons chopped garlic

Add mushrooms, peas and garlic, cover partially and cook, stirring occasionally, for 3 minutes.

- 2 tablespoons tomato paste
- 400 grams tomatoes, diced
- ¼ cup chopped fresh basil
- 1½ tablespoons balsamic vinegar
- 1 teaspoon chopped fresh thyme
- Salt to taste
- Black pepper powder to taste

Add tomato paste and cook 2 minutes. Add tomatoes, basil, vinegar, thyme, salt and pepper powder and mix well.

Bring the mixture to a simmer, cover partially and cook gently for 3-4 minutes. Transfer the mixture into the prepared pie pan or casserole.

- 5 cups roughly chopped boiled potatoes
- 1 cup warm soy milk
- 3 tablespoons canola oil

Take potatoes in a mixing bowl, add soy milk and canola oil gradually and mash.

Spread this mixture evenly over the filling in the pie pan or casserole. Place the pan or casserole in the preheated oven and bake 15 minutes, or till it is bubbling hot. Cool for 5 minutes before serving.

SPIRULINA SMOOTHIE

PREPARATION TIME : 5 MINUTES
SERVES : 1-2

V GF

- 1 teaspoon spirulina
- 2 cups almond milk or coconut milk
- 1 ripe banana, peeled and sliced
- 1 cup chopped pineapple
- 1 cup greens (kale / spinach)
- 2 tablespoons hemp seeds or flax seeds
- 1 tablespoon chia seeds
- 4-5 fresh mint leaves

Put spirulina, almond milk or coconut milk, banana, pineapple, greens, hemp seeds, chia seeds and mint leaves into a blender jar and blend till well combined.

Pour into individual glasses and serve.

SOBA IN TAHINI SAUCE

PREPARATION TIME : 10 MINUTES
SERVES : 3-4

V GF

225 grams or 1 cup soba noodles (noodles made with buckwheat flour or kuttu ka atta)
Sea salt, to taste

$\frac{1}{3}$ cup tahini
2 tablespoons rice vinegar
1 tablespoon finely grated fresh ginger
1 tablespoon white miso
2 teaspoons soy sauce
1 teaspoon sesame oil
A handful fresh coriander leaves, chopped
A pinch of red chilli flakes

---

1 large or 2 small cucumbers
1 bunch spring onions, chopped
2 tablespoons sesame seeds (preferably black)
Sea salt, to taste

Take sufficient water in a deep non-stick pan, add salt and bring it to a boil. Add soba noodles and cook till al dente. Drain.

While the noodles are boiling, whisk together tahini, rice vinegar, ginger, miso, soy sauce, sesame oil, half the coriander leaves and red chilli flakes in a medium bowl. Once blended, add $\frac{1}{3}$ - $\frac{1}{2}$ cup water to reach the desired consistency and whisk well.

Toss the soba noodles in this sauce.

Slice cucumber into thin, long strips. Add the cucumber strips, spring onions, sesame seeds and remaining coriander leaves and toss well. Serve immediately.

A GUT FEELING
(from left to right)
BANANA SLICES WITH PEANUT BUTTER

A Gut Feeling, trust it

The gut produces neurotransmitters like serotonin, dopamine and ghrelin, which are important in controlling our mood, motivation levels and appetite.

Few of us give enough attention to our gut and its bacteria, which line our intestines and help to digest food. During digestion, the bacteria makes vitamins that are vital for life and makes small molecules that can help your brain work. However, not all gut bacteria is good. Certain bacteria can strengthen the immune system, while others can promote inflammation.

Anxiety influences the gut and at the same time a distressed gut can cause stress and anxiety. Maintaining a healthy balance of good and bad bacteria, acids and alkalis may play a role in reducing inflammation and may help burn body fat and reduce insulin resistance.

We can change the bacteria within through our food intake. Prebiotic and probiotic foods can alter the flora in the gut by increasing the growth of healthy bacteria. Kefir increases vitamin K which prevents bone cells from dying.

What we feed our stomach we also feed our brain.

Strengthen the gut by using:

- Supplements like glutamine, magnesium, vitamin A
- With pre and probiotic foods and supplements
- Digestive enzymes, vitamin B6 and zinc along with the digestive enzyme help it to work better
- Antioxidants to boost the immune system

POSITIVE TAKEAWAYS

+ Gut brain influences thinking brain
+ Certain foods help change the bacteria
+ Have prebiotic and probiotic foods

PREBIOTIC	PROBIOTIC
Act as a fertilizer for the good bacteria that's already there --- They are specialised plant fibre --- Consuming prebiotics on a daily basis leads to reduced anxiety, depression, and stress --- Onions, Garlic, Asparagus, Artichoke, Seaweed, Flax seeds, Mushrooms, Aloe Vera, Endive, Dandelion Greens, Leeks, Chives, Kale, Spinach, Bananas, Kiwi, Apples, Bel (wood apple), Barley, Oats, Beans and Sprouts	Introduce good bacteria into the gut --- They are live bacteria. The process of fermentation produces probiotics --- They are effective during pregnancy and breast feeding, as they stimulate production of immuno-globulin, which strengthens the immune systems --- Kimchi, Sauerkraut, Lacto-fermented pickles, Miso, Tempeh, Buttermilk, Yogurt, Kefir, Soft cheeses, Spirulina, Carrots, Beets, Sourdough bread.

Note: Adding sugar to yogurt changes the probiotic bacteria to bad bacteria.

BANANA SLICES WITH PEANUT BUTTER

PREPARATION TIME : 5 MINUTES
SERVES : 1-2

Ingredients	Method
1 ripe banana 1-2 tablespoons peanut butter	Peel banana. Spread some peanut butter over half the banana.
1-2 tablespoons hemp seeds or 1-2 tablespoons flax seeds and sesame seeds	Sprinkle hemp seeds or flax and sesame seeds on top and slice into bite-sized pieces.
Honey, as required (optional)	Drizzle a little honey if you want it to be sweeter. *Optional : Add salt and lemon juice for a sweet sour taste.*

KIMCHI

PREPARATION TIME : 1 HOUR + 10 MINUTES + 2 DAYS (TO FERMENT)
MAKES : 2-3 CUPS

- 1 medium cabbage
- 4 tablespoons sea salt

Chop the cabbage into 4cm pieces and place it in a large bowl. Sprinkle salt all over it.

Cover the cabbage with cold water. Set aside for 1 hour.

Put the cabbage in a colander and rinse thoroughly under cold running water to remove excess salt. Leave it in the colander to drain excess water.

- 6 garlic cloves
- A thumb-sized piece of ginger, peeled
- 2 teaspoons caster sugar
- 2 tablespoons Korean shrimp paste (vegetarians can omit)
- 2 tablespoons soy sauce
- 5 tablespoons fish sauce or vegetarian oyster sauce
- 3 tablespoons red chilli powder

- 200 grams radish (daikon), cut into thin strips
- 6 spring onions, cut into thin strips

Blend together garlic, ginger and sugar to a smooth paste. Transfer it into a bowl and add shrimp paste, soy sauce, vegetarian oyster sauce or fish sauce and chilli powder and mix.

Add radish and spring onions. Squeeze out any excess water from the cabbage and add it to the bowl. Mix thoroughly.

Spoon the kimchi into a large jar and press it down so that the juices rise. Leave a gap at the top, then close and seal the lid.

Leave the kimchi to ferment at room temperature for 4–5 days.
Check the kimchi every day, letting out some gas and pressing the vegetables down. When the kimchi tastes delicious, keep the jar in the fridge. This will keep it fresh for up to 3 months.

A GUT FEELING

(from left to right)

ASIAN FISH CURRY

TOFU STEAK WITH SHIITAKE MUSHROOMS

KIMCHI

ASIAN FISH CURRY

PREPARATION TIME : 15-20 MINUTES
SERVES : 4

1 tablespoons vegetable oil
1 garlic clove, sliced
Green parts of 4 young leeks or 2 stalks spring onion greens, finely chopped

1 teaspoon coriander powder
1 teaspoon cumin powder
¼ fresh red chilli, seeded and very finely sliced
1 teaspoon turmeric powder
2 one-inch pieces fresh ginger, peeled and grated finely

---

10 cherry tomatoes, roughly quartered
1 stalk of lemongrass, very finely chopped
165 grams coconut milk
2 kaffir lime leaves

---

1 tablespoon fresh lemon juice
A pinch of sugar
Salt to taste
Black pepper powder to taste
A dash of fish sauce (optional)

---

400 grams white fish, cut into small chunks or a mix of white fish and prawns

---

1 tablespoon chopped fresh coriander leaves

Heat vegetable oil in a non-stick wok or a large non-stick frying pan, add garlic and sauté gently till light brown. Add spring onion greens and sauté till soft, but not discoloured.

Add coriander powder, cumin powder, red chilli, turmeric powder and ginger and sauté gently for 1 minute.

Add tomatoes, lemongrass, coconut milk and kaffir lime leaves.

Mix well and simmer gently for about 5 minutes.

Add lemon juice, sugar, salt and pepper powder. Add fish sauce, if you want to add more flavour to the curry. If your curry needs a little more liquid add a little water.

Add fish and cook for 6-8 minutes or till the fish is done.

Garnish with coriander leaves and serve hot with steamed rice.

TOFU STEAK WITH SHIITAKE MUSHROOMS

PREPARATION TIME : 15 MINUTES
SERVES : 4

V GF

- 400 grams extra-firm tofu, drained
- 3 tablespoons sesame oil
- 3 tablespoons soy sauce

Cut tofu in half crosswise and again in half lengthwise. Pierce tofu liberally with a fork. Place in a shallow dish. Take 1 tablespoon oil and 1 tablespoon soy sauce in a small bowl, mix well and pour this mixture over tofu and let stand for 15 minutes.

- 1 cup thin strips of red capsicums
- 1 cup thin strips of carrot
- Salt to taste

Heat 1 tablespoon oil in a large non-stick pan over medium-high heat. Add capsicum, carrot and salt and sauté 3 minutes. Transfer into another bowl.

- 4 garlic cloves, thinly sliced
- 140 grams shiitake mushrooms, sliced
- ½ cup vegetable broth
- 1 tablespoon honey
- 2 teaspoons sherry/wine vinegar
- ½ teaspoon crushed peppercorns

Add remaining 1 tablespoon oil to the same pan. Add garlic and mushrooms and sauté for 4 minutes.
Add remaining 2 tablespoons soy sauce, vegetable broth, honey, vinegar and crushed peppercorns and mix well.

Simmer 3 minutes or till the mixture thickens. Remove the pan from heat. Remove tofu from marinade and reserve the marinade.

Heat a non-stick grill pan over high heat. Place the tofu steaks in the pan and grill for 3 minutes on each side, adding the reserved marinade a few times.

Place 1 tofu steak on each of 4 plates, top each serving with about ¼ cup carrot mixture and about 2 tablespoons mushroom mixture and serve immediately.

DETOX
(from left to right)
COCONUT BASIL STIR-FRY
RED PEPPER & CILANTRO DIP
BORSCHT

Detox,
a way of life

A detox diet aims to clean and eliminate toxins from the body. Toxins slow down your metabolism and cause headaches, acidity, fatigue, stiffness, bloating. They place severe stress on the organs of elimination and weaken the immune system. Which is why, after a detox, when your body is free of excess toxins, you tend to feel lighter and more energetic.

The gut and liver are your two primary detox organs. The gut produces 70% of the antibodies and contains the greatest lymphocytes in the body. The lymph contains infection-fighting white blood cells that help the body to get rid of toxins, waste and other unwanted materials.

The liver is responsible for processing nutrients absorbed from the small intestine. It clears the blood and body of toxins like drugs, chemicals from medication, fertilizers, additives, preservatives, alcohol, cigarettes, car exhaust and aerosol sprays and also removes dead cells.

Treat your liver and gut with care. Eat a good, well balanced nourishing diet. Drink plenty of water. There are no short cuts. You know that you are winning when the improved feeling of health in your body outweighs the urge to eat too much of the wrong kinds of food.

Some foods that help the liver:

- Garlic, onions, ginger and turmeric
- Broccoli, cauliflower, bean sprouts, brussel sprouts
- Green leafy vegetables, kale
- Beetroots, carrots, pumpkins, artichokes, asparagus,
- Lemons, grapefruits, apples
- Green tea, camomile & herbal teas
- Wheatgrass, spirulina, aloe vera
- Olive oil, avocado
  Walnuts (rich in omega 3 fats)
- Quinoa, buckwheat, millets, oats

POSITIVE TAKEAWAYS

+ Toxins weaken immunity
+ Gut and liver detoxify

BORSCHT (RUSSIAN-STYLE BEET SOUP)

PREPARATION TIME : 20 MINUTES
SERVES : 6-8

V GF

- 2 tablespoons light olive oil
- 1 bay leaf
- 8 cups vegetable stock

Heat oil in a non-stick pan over medium-high heat. Add bay leaf and 4 cups vegetable stock and bring to a boil. Cover the pot, turn heat down and simmer, stirring occasionally.

- 800 grams beetroots, scrubbed

Shred 1/3 of the beets and finely chop the remaining 2/3. Add finely chopped beet to the pot, bring the mixture to a boil, cover the pot and cook for 10 minutes.

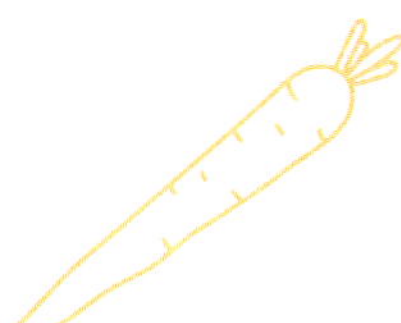

- 4 medium carrots, finely chopped
- 3 large stalks of celery, diced
- 1 large onion, chopped
- 1 large potato, scrubbed and chopped
- 225 grams cabbage, shredded
- 4 large garlic cloves, minced
- 1/2 teaspoon coarse salt
- 1/4 teaspoon black pepper powder
- 1/4 teaspoon ground allspice (cinnamon, clove, nutmeg)
- 3 tablespoons tomato paste

Add shredded beet, carrots, celery, onion, potato, cabbage, garlic, coarse salt, black pepper powder, allspice, tomato paste and remaining 4 cups stock (if required, depending on the consistency you like).

Cover the pot and bring the mixture to a boil again, Turn the heat down and simmer till the vegetables are tender.

- 6 tablespoons red wine vinegar or apple cider vinegar

Add vinegar, then turn off the heat and stir in the dill. Taste and add additional salt and pepper as desired.

- 1/4 cup chopped fresh dill for garnish
- Yogurt, preferably thick hung curd, for garnish (optional)

To serve, ladle the soup into bowls. Top with a dollop of yogurt and a sprinkling of fresh dill. Serve cold.

RED PEPPER & CILANTRO DRESSING

PREPARATION TIME : UNDER 10 MINUTES
MAKES : 1 CUP

V GF

- 1/2 medium red capsicum, chopped roughly
- 3/4 cup fresh coriander leaves
- 1 small tomato
- 1 garlic clove
- 1 1/2 tablespoons lemon juice
- 1/2 teaspoon salt
- 1/4 teaspoon black pepper powder
- 1/2 teaspoon miso paste (optional)
- 1 teaspoon apple cider vinegar

Blend together red capsicum, coriander leaves, tomato, garlic, lemon juice, salt, 1 tablespoon water, black pepper powder, miso paste (if using) and apple cider vinegar till well combined.

Pour into a bowl and use as required. You can serve it fresh, or store up to 2 days in the refrigerator.

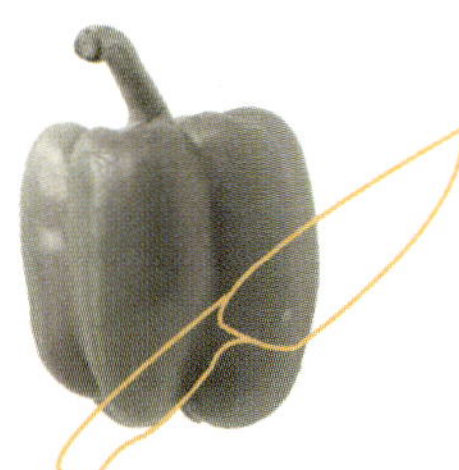

COCONUT BASIL STIR-FRY

PREPARATION TIME : 10 MINUTES
SERVES : 4

V GF

1 cup coconut milk
1 cup chopped fresh basil leaves
1 tablespoon fresh lemon juice
2 tablespoons rice vinegar
1 teaspoon arrowroot powder or rice flour
1 tablespoon maple syrup

---

1 tablespoon coconut oil
2 garlic cloves, minced
1/4 cup diced onion
1 teaspoon grated fresh ginger

1/2 cup bean sprouts
4 medium carrots, halved vertically and cut into 1/4 inch thick diagonal slices
1 red capsicum, cut into strips
1 cup thinly sliced mushrooms
1 cup broccoli florets
1 cup thinly sliced bok choy or cabbage

Salt to taste
2 teaspoons red chilli powder

2 cups cooked quinoa or black rice

To make coconut basil sauce, put coconut milk, basil leaves, lemon juice, rice vinegar, arrowroot powder or rice flour and maple syrup in a blender jar and blend well. Transfer into a bowl and set aside.

For stir-fry, heat oil in a large non-stick wok over medium-high heat, add garlic and onion and sauté till translucent. Add ginger and sauté for another minute.

Add bean sprouts, carrots, capsicum and mushrooms and sauté for 3 minutes. Add broccoli and bok choy and mix.

Add salt and chilli powder and toss well.

Pour the coconut sauce over the vegetables and mix lightly. Reduce heat, cover and cook, stirring occasionally, for a few minutes or till the sauce begins to thicken. Do not overcook.

Serve over quinoa or black rice.

ALLERGIES
(from left to right)
POTATO, KALE & BEAN SOUP
ZUCCHINI NOODLES

Allergies, work your way out

Did you know that some food allergies are temporary while others are permanent?

Many people suffer from food allergies. A food allergy is when your body treats the food as an invader and thus attacks it and attempts to destroy it.

The WBC's (white blood cells), also known as the fighter cells and protective cells of the body are collectively sent to remove the allergen. Bloating of the stomach is due to the collective release of the WBC's.

Side effects of this battle within may cause rhinitis, sinusitis, constipation, diarrhea, skin rash etc.

A food allergy may develop because:

- The food contains certain proteins that the body does not like
- Due to the lack of sufficient digestive enzymes
- Excessive antibiotics, alcohol, stress, gut infection
- Due to a zinc deficiency

Allergies are of 2 types:

Those in which the reaction is within minutes or upto 2 hours of having the food (IGE) and the other in which the reaction to the food can take up to 48 hours to show up (IGG).

Most of the IGE allergies are genetic. Symptoms show up on skin, gut and airways. The IGE foods have to be completely eliminated from your diet.

In IGG food allergies, the immune system reacts to the allergen especially when there is an overabundance of the allergen. IGG allergies can be reversed over a period of time.

Thus the process of treating food allergies is discovering the food that triggers the allergy, eliminating it from the diet for about 6 months. Cleaning the gut and strengthening the immune system in these 6 months. Then reintroducing the foods and testing the reaction. If there is no reaction on consuming the food repetitively, then desensitization has happened.

Sensitivity to chemicals such as food additives, colouring, flavouring and pollutants, may trigger a reaction similar to an allergic reaction.

Some foods that help fight allergies and inflammation are:

- Kiwi, apples, pineapple, oranges, berries
- Red onions, spinach, carrots, broccoli, capsicums
- Ginger, garlic
- Flax seeds, pumpkin seeds, sunflower seeds, walnuts

POSITIVE TAKEAWAYS

+ Identify triggers
+ Eliminate them from diet for 6 weeks
+ Reintroduce the food.

ZUCCHINI NOODLES

PREPARATION TIME : 15 MINUTES
SERVES : 4 (CONTAINS NUTS)

V GF

3 large bunches basil (or about 1-1½ cups packed basil leaves)
2 garlic cloves
2 tablespoons olive oil
½ cup roughly chopped walnuts
½ tablespoon white wine vinegar
Salt to taste
Black pepper powder to taste

To make pesto, put basil leaves, garlic, olive oil, walnuts, 2 tablespoons water, white wine vinegar, salt and black pepper powder in a blender jar and blend. If the sauce is too thick, gradually add more water.

---

4 zucchini
2 tablespoons lemon juice

To make zucchini noodles, gently run the julienne peeler over the zucchini (with skin on) until strings of noodles come off. Place them in a large bowl. Add a little lemon juice and toss to prevent them from browning.

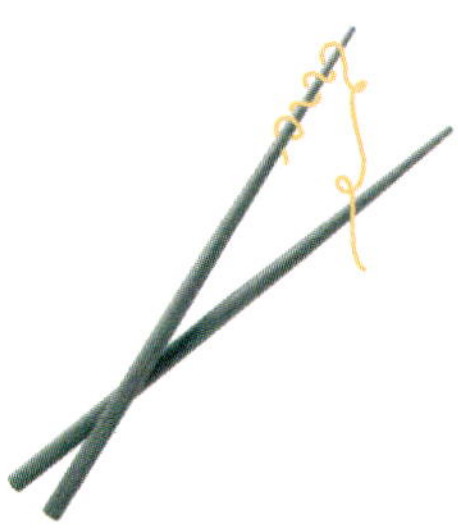

½ tablespoon oil
1 garlic clove

Heat oil in a non-stick pan, add garlic and sauté till fragrant. Add zucchini noodles and toss.

Cook till they are slightly tender but not soft. The zucchini will lose its crunchiness if overcooked.

½ cup cherry tomatoes, halved
Sea salt to taste
2 cups shredded spinach

Add cherry tomatoes, salt and spinach and toss. Add pesto sauce and mix.

---

2 tablespoons sunflower seeds

Garnish with sunflower seeds.
Serve hot as a main course or serve cold as a salad.

POTATO, KALE & BEAN SOUP

PREPARATION TIME : 15-20 MINUTES
SERVES : 4

V GF

2 cups chopped onions
6 garlic cloves, minced

Put onions in a large non-stick pot, add 1 tablespoon water and cook till the onions are soft. Add garlic and cook for 1 minute more.

8 cups vegetable broth
450 grams small potatoes, diced into bite-sized pieces
23 cups of black or white beans
1 teaspoon of dried oregano
1 teaspoon dried basil
½ teaspoon dried rosemary, crushed
½ teaspoon fennel seeds
¼ - ½ teaspoon of red chilli flakes (less if you like it less spicy)
Salt to taste

Add broth, potatoes, beans, oregano, dried basil, dried rosemary, fennel seeds, red chilli flakes and salt and let the mixture come to a boil. Reduce heat, cover and simmer till the potatoes and beans are soft.

---

25 grams kale, stems trimmed and leaves chopped

Add kale, cover, and cook for another 5 minutes. The kale should be tender but still bright green.

For a thicker consistency, mash some of the potatoes.
Serve with warm bread.

Note:
If available, use fresh herbs in place of dried herb.

GLUTEN ALLERGY

CEVICHE

Gluten Allergy,
celiac disease

Celiac disease, the reason behind your gluten-free fad, is an autoimmune disorder where the ingestion of gluten leads to damage in the small intestine. It is hereditary.

Symptoms include bloating, cramping, constipation or diarrhea, bone or joint pain, headaches, fatigue, itching and hives.

Gluten is a protein that is commonly found in wheat, rye, barley. People suffering from celiac disease may also be affected by oats, since it contains a protein very similar to gluten.

5-7% Type 1 diabetics have gluten intolerance. Both are autoimmune diseases and have a similar genetic basis.

POSITIVE TAKEAWAYS

+ Autoimmune disease
+ Gluten damages small intestine
+ Alcohols also contain gluten

AVOID	HAVE
Wheat, Barley, Rye Malt Brewers' yeast Oats Pasta, Bread, Biscuits (unless gluten-free) Semolina, Durum flour, Couscous, Spelt, Graham flour are all wheat based	Rice Corn Jowar (sorghum) Millets like Bajra (pearl millet) and Ragi (finger millet) Quinoa Kuttu (buckwheat) Rajgira (amaranth) Soy

Note: Be aware that many alcohols are made from wheat, rye or barley, especially whisky, beer and many vodkas.

CARROT CAKE

PREPARATION + COOKING TIME : 10 + 20 MINUTES
SERVES : 4-6

GF

Preheat the oven to 350°F/180°C. Grease a cake tin.

- 1 teaspoon dried yeast

Mix yeast with 2 tablespoons warm water in a small bowl and set aside to prove.

- 3 large eggs
- 1/2 cup vegetable oil or coconut milk
- 1 cup brown sugar or jaggery

Break the eggs into a mixing bowl and whisk. Add oil and continue to whisk. Add brown sugar and beat till smooth.

- 1/3 cup plain yogurt
- 2 teaspoons vanilla extract
- 1 tablespoon honey or agave (for added moisture)
- Juice of 1/2 orange
- 1/2 teaspoon grated ginger
- 1 teaspoon cinnamon powder
- 1 teaspoon mixture of nutmeg powder, clove powder, dried ginger powder, allspice powder

Beat in the yogurt, vanilla extract, honey, orange juice, ginger, cinnamon powder and mixed spice powders.

- 2 cups sorghum (jowar) flour or rice flour

Add flour, yeast and beat till combined.

- 3/4 cup descicated coconut
- 1 1/2 cups finely grated carrots
- 1/2 cup toasted chopped walnuts or pecans (optional)

Add coconut, carrots, and nuts and mix with a wooden spoon.

Spread the batter evenly in the cake tin, place the tin in the preheated oven and bake for 20-25 minutes or till the cake is firm.

Take the tin out of the oven and let it cool down to room temperature.

Demould, slice and serve.

CEVICHE

PREPARATION TIME : 3.5 HOURS
SERVES : 6-8

GF

700 grams seafood, diced (such as shrimp, scallops, yellow tail, tilapia or any other locally available fish)
1/2 cup freshly squeezed lemon juice
1/4 cup freshly squeezed orange juice

2-3 medium tomatoes, diced
1 large onion, diced
2 medium cucumbers, diced
1 fresh sweet corn cob, kernels separated
4 garlic cloves, minced
1 fresh jalapeño, seeded and minced or green chilli
1/2 cup chopped fresh coriander leaves + for garnishing
2 tablespoons extra virgin olive oil
1/2 cup Sriracha or hot chilli sauce
1 cup tomato juice

Salt to taste
Freshly ground black pepper powder

---

1 avocado, sliced, for garnish

Take the seafood in a large bowl, add lemon juice and orange juice and mix. Cover and keep the bowl in the refrigerator, stirring occasionally, for 3 hours or till the flesh becomes firm and opaque.

Add tomatoes, onion, cucumbers, corn, garlic, jalapeño, coriander leaves, extra virgin olive oil, chilli sauce and tomato juice and mix well. Cover and refrigerate for another 30 minutes to allow the flavours to blend.

Season with salt and pepper to taste.

Serve in chilled bowls or martini glasses, garnished with avocado slices and coriander leaves.

Note:
If serving with chips, look for gluten content. Use baked corn or potato chips.

LACTOSE INTOLERANCE

TOFU BHURJI

Lactose Intolerance, the dairy allergy

Did you know that as you age, your ability to digest dairy products diminishes? Lactose intolerance occurs because a person lacks the enzyme lactase, which is needed to break down dairy. You may not realize that you are lactose intolerant, so watch out for some of its symptoms which include bloating, flatulence, indigestion, constipation, acidity, running nose, sneezing and hives. A simple skin test or blood test can determine if you are lactose intolerant.

Fortunately, there are many easily available substitutes to milk. Dairy free cheese is also available in many supermarkets or online. Most places in the world have easy access to lactose free milk.

Soy milk is a good source of complete protein which also provides the necessary calcium. Tofu, a food cultivated by coagulating soy milk, can easily replace paneer in their diet. Those with a family history of breast cancer need to have it in limited portions as it is very high in estrogen. Also it is not suitable for thyroid patients.

Almond milk is a very low calorie supplement to dairy milk. This milk is rich in vitamin A, D, E and provides good fat compared to dairy milk.

Rice milk is the least allergenic milk and is therefore suits most people. It is the sweetest of all non-dairy milks. Ofcourse it is a low protein, carbohydrate based milk. Diabetics need to avoid it.

Coconut milk is high in good fat (medium chain MCFA) and has anti-viral and antibacterial properties. The fat from coconut milk is metabolized quickly into energy and thus does not get stored as fat.

Hemp milk is creamy and nutty in taste. It is high in calcium, phosphorus and vitamin D and B12. Its benefits include strengthened immune system and increased mental capacity.

Quinoa milk is high in calcium and potassium. It is good for skin and hair conditioning and also has anti-inflammatory properties.

Oat milk has a mild oaty flavour. It is high in fibre, folic acid, vitamin E and phytochemicals that could help prevent heart disease, stroke and some types of cancer.

Goat's milk contains proteins and fats different from those present in cow's milk, making it easier for some people to digest. Thus lactose intolerant people may tolerate goat's milk and goat cheese. It contains as much potassium, magnesium, iron and calcium as cow's milk.

Unpasteurized milk is a health hazard because of the dangers of bacterial diseases.

POSITIVE TAKEAWAYS

+ Lactose digesting enzymes diminish with age
+ Get a skin or blood test to check for lactose intolerance
+ Substitute dairy with soy, almond, rice, coconut, hemp or quinoa milk

CHOCOLATE MOUSSE

PREPARATION TIME : 5 MINUTES
SERVES : 3

100 grams dark chocolate
+ 25 grams for decoration

2 tablespoons maple syrup or honey
2 teaspoons vanilla bean paste or extract
5 tablespoons almond milk or coconut milk
1/4 teaspoon salt

Set aside the 25 grams of chocolate for decoration and break the rest into squares and put into a bowl.

Melt the chocolate over a double boiler whisking it continuously. Add maple syrup, vanilla, almond or coconut milk, salt and whisk till smooth.

Divide the mixture equally between 3 small serving glasses (80ml). Chill for about 3 hours.

To decorate, scrape the edge of the reserved chocolate with a vegetable peeler to make long shards. Scatter them over the mousse just before serving.

Note:
The consistency is like that of thick chocolate sauce. If you want it to set like a mousse then add a piece of avocado. The avocado will set it.

TOFU BHURJI

PREPARATION TIME : UNDER 10 MINUTES
SERVES : 2-3

GF

200 gram extra-firm tofu	Crumble the tofu and keep aside in a bowl.
1½ tablespoons oil ½ teaspoon cumin seeds 1 medium onion, finely chopped	Heat oil in a non-stick frying pan. Add cumin seeds and when they turn brown, add onion and sauté till soft.
½ inch ginger, finely chopped 1 green chilli, finely chopped	Add ginger and green chilli and sauté for a few seconds.
1 large tomato, finely chopped	Add tomato and sauté till tomato becomes soft.
Pinch of turmeric powder Pinch of red chilli powder ¼ teaspoon garam masala powder (optional) Salt to taste 1 tablespoon chopped fresh coriander leaves	Add turmeric powder, red chilli powder, and garam masala powder and mix. Add crumbled tofu and mix well. Sauté for 3-4 minutes. Season with salt. Add coriander leaves and mix. Serve hot.

QUINOA MILK

PREPARATION TIME : 10-15 MINUTES
MAKES : 800 ML APPROX

V GF

Ingredients	Method
1 cup cooked quinoa (240grams)	Presoak the quinoa and cook it.
3 cups water (750ml)	Blend the quinoa with the water until well blended and almost smooth.
	Strain the blended quinoa mixture. Can use it unstrained too.
4 dates 1/4 teaspoon cinnamon	Pour the quinoa milk in a blender and blend with the dates and cinnamon.
	Store the quinoa milk in a sealed container in the fridge for 3 or 4 days.

STEAMED SALMON & ASPARAGUS

PREPARATION TIME : 10 MINUTES
SERVES : 4

GF

Take lightly salted water in a steamer with tight fitting lid and bring it a boil.

2 bunches asparagus,
bottom hard part trimmed

When water comes to a boil, place asparagus in the steamer basket, cover, and cook for 3-5 minutes or till asparagus is tender.

2 tablespoons fresh lemon juice
1/2 tablespoon extra-virgin olive oil
Salt to taste
White pepper powder to taste

Remove asparagus from steamer and toss it with 1 tablespoon lemon juice, 1/2 tablespoon olive oil, salt and pepper powder.

Mustard dill sauce
1 tablespoon Dijon mustard sauce
4 tablespoons chopped fresh dill
100 grams silken tofu
1 tablespoon honey
1 tablespoon fresh lemon juice
Salt to taste
1/4 teaspoon white pepper powder
1 tablespoons extra virgin olive oil

To make mustard dill sauce, put Dijon mustard sauce, dill, tofu, honey, 1 tablespoon lemon juice, 1/2 cup water, salt and white pepper powder in a blender and blend at high speed for about 1 minute. While the blender is running, pour olive oil, a little at a time, and continue to blend. Transfer into a bowl and set aside.

700 grams salmon fillets,
skin and bones removed
and cut into 4 pieces
Black pepper powder to taste

Rub salmon with 1 tablespoon lemon juice and season with a little salt and black pepper powder.

Note:
Vegetarians can replace salmon
for tofu or cottage cheese.

Place salmon in the same steamer basket and steam for 3-4 minutes or till pink inside.

Place salmon on a plate and keep the asparagus by its side. Pour desired amount of sauce over it and the asparagus. Serve.

MILLENNIAL CONCERNS

(from left to right)
BARBECUED FISH WITH AVOCADO & BANANA
ALMOND MILK KHEER

Stress,
a part of everyday life

At a basic level, the body releases hormones to combat stress, speeding up the heart rate and pumping blood faster to carry sugar and oxygen to the brain and muscles. Stress is associated with a rise in cholesterol levels and slowing down of digestion. It wears out our immune system. Constant stimulation of the nervous system causes hormonal imbalance and weight gain.

Due to increased levels of cortisol, the stress hormone, stressed people tend to crave junk foods, mainly high in carbohydrates, sugar and fats. These foods leaves us feeling good for a while and then guilty for the extra calories consumed. A healthy diet can help counter the impact of stress by strengthening the immune system.

POSITIVE TAKEAWAYS

+ Increased blood sugar, heart rate
+ Lowered immunity
+ Exercise is the best cure

To deal with stress:

- Replace caffeine with herbal teas.

- Have turmeric as it support the production of new brain cells during stress and boosts lymphatic circulation.

- Have tulsi (holy basil) because it balances cortisol, the stress hormone.

- Eat fruits to satisfy your sugar cravings.

- Have almonds, citrus fruits and foods high in Vitamin A, C, E as they are rich in antioxidants.

- Consume vitamin B rich foods like peanuts since they calm the brain by cutting levels of cortisol and adrenaline, and boosting serotonin levels.

- Have magnesium rich foods like spinach, soy beans or salmon to fight fatigue and headaches, and potassium rich foods like avocado or coconut water to soothe the nerves.

- Exercise because physical exertion helps burn all the sugar and fats released in order to escape stress.

- Another bedtime stress buster is the time-honoured glass of warm milk. Research shows that calcium eases anxiety and mood swings.

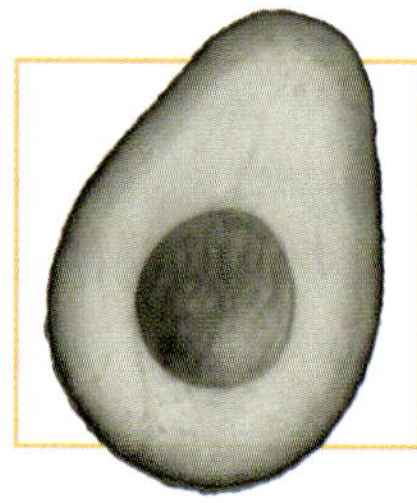

ALMOND MILK KHEER (RICE PUDDING)

PREPARATION TIME : 20 MINUTES
SERVES : 6-8

V GF

100 grams rice A pinch of salt	Boil 150 grams water in a deep non-stick pan, add salt and rice and cook for 3 minutes, until there is little or no water left. The rice will be partially cooked.
1 litre almond milk 1 vanilla pod or 2 teaspoons vanilla essence 5-6 saffron threads 1 inch cinnamon stick or 1/2 teaspoon cinnamon powder	Take almond milk in another deep non-stick pan, add vanilla pod and saffron and simmer. After the milk starts boiling, add the cinnamon and rice. Cook over very low heat until rice is soft. Turn off the gas.
100 grams jaggery 5 green cardamom pods or 1 teaspoon green cardamom powder	Add jaggery and green cardamom powder and mix. The jaggery will melt in the hot kheer.
	Remove the vanilla pod. At the end of cooking, the mixture should have sufficient liquid. On cooling, the rice will continue to absorb the almond milk and become smooth. If you cook for longer, when cooled the mixture may become too thick. In such a case add more almond milk to get the right consistency.
Crushed pistachios for garnishing	Garnish with crushed pistachios and serve at room temperature.

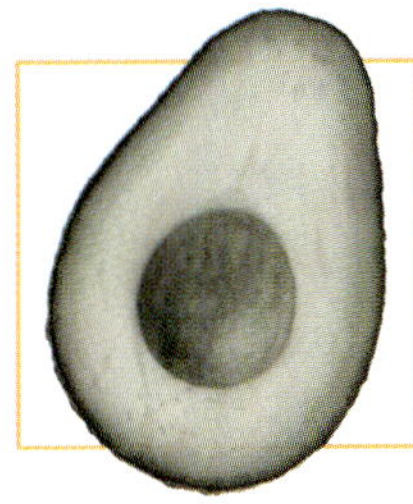

BARBECUED FISH WITH AVOCADO & BANANA

PREPARATION TIME : 10 MINUTES
SERVES : 4

1 kg fish, scaled, gutted and fins also removed 4 slices lemon or 1 lemon Salt to taste	Rub salt and lemon on the fish and leave it to marinate for an hour.
--- 2 large ripe avocados	Cut the avocados in half lengthways and remove the stone. Rub some lemon to prevent it from getting black.
1 medium ripe banana, sliced into 1 cm pieces 4 tablespoons honey	Cook banana with a little salt in a non-stick pan till nicely coloured and slightly soft. Add honey.
3 garlic cloves, finely chopped 4 tablespoons parsley, chopped fresh Black pepper powder to taste Juice of 1 large lemons	Scoop the avocados. Mix the banana mixture with the avocado. Add garlic, parsley, salt and pepper, lemon juice and stir it in.
	Fill the halved avocados with the banana and avocado stirred mixture.
2 sprigs of fresh coriander leaves 2 sprigs of fresh rosemary 2-3 spring onions, chopped	Make slits in the sides of the fillet. Stuff coriander leaves, rosemary and spring onion into the side of the fish.
	Cook the fish over the barbecue or grill.
	Put the barbecued fish on top of the stuffed avocado.
1 tablespoon olive oil	Sprinkle with salt, pepper, lime and a little olive oil.

HANGOVER

(from left to right)

HUEVOS RANCHEROS

FRENCH TOAST

Hangover, do the cures really work?

Did you know that the medical term for a hangover is "veisalgia"? It represents all those unpleasant symptoms like dizziness, fatigue, headache, nausea and a dry mouth, that some of us might be all too familiar with after a night of heavy drinking. The primary reason you feel hung over is due to dehydration, and the presence of alcoholic toxins in your bloodstream. The stomach lining is disrupted due to an overproduction of acids.

Hangovers cause blood sugar levels to drop, which can lead to fatigue and shakiness. Alcohol causes the depletion of vitamin C, as well as B6 and folic acid. Heavy drinking depletes the electrolytes (calcium, sodium and magnesium).

To avoid hangovers:
Line your stomach with a balanced meal of carbohydrates and proteins before drinking. Opt for a peanut butter sandwich with a green leafy salad and chickpeas or tofu. Have an apple and water before sleeping.

After the hangover:
- Start the day with a glass of coconut water, which is a natural electrolyte. Replenish your vitamin C with a lime/ lemon shot or orange juice.

- The best detox drink is vegetable juice made with bottle gourd (lauki) or rigde gourd(torai)/ cucumber and lemon. Do not add salt.

- Breakfast with eggs and toast of whole wheat bread (avoid butter, because fats need more water to digest, and the body is already dehydrated from excess alcohol).

- For a change a cup of strong coffee is desirable, so enjoy your 1 cup of coffee. Rest of the day sip on herbal tea and snack on bananas and dates.

- There is no better cure than sleep and drinking lots of water.

Some cures from all over the world:

- Bowl of hearty spicy soup
- Cup of espresso
- Coconut water
- Fruit juice, tomato juice, cabbage juice
- Plain starchy foods like toast, noodles, potatoes and rice
- Bananas, dates and leafy greens

POSITIVE TAKEAWAYS

+ Alcohol depletes electrolytes
+ Hangovers cause drop in blood sugar
+ Water and sleep are the best cures

HUEVOS RANCHEROS

PREPARATION TIME : 25 MINUTES
SERVES : 4

- 3 tablespoons oil
- 1 medium onion, finely chopped
- 1 garlic clove, chopped
- 2 green chillies, seeded and finely chopped

- 1 medium red capsicum, chopped

- 2 cups chopped tomatoes
- 1 cup tomato purée
- 1 teaspoon red chilli powder
- Ground cumin to taste (optional)

- Juice of 1 lemon
- Salt to taste
- Black pepper powder to taste

- 4 eggs

- 4 corn tortillas (thin corn roti)
- Fresh marjoram or fresh basil leaves, to garnish

Heat 1 tablespoon oil in a large non-stick pan, add onion and sauté till soft but not browned.

Add garlic and chillies and sauté.

Add capsicum and sauté.

Add tomatoes, tomato purée, chilli powder, cumin and continue to sauté on low heat for 10 minutes.

Season with lemon juice, salt and pepper powder.

Heat a little of the remaining oil in another non-stick pan for each egg, and fry them, one at a time.

Put a tortilla in a bowl, then put the egg and top it with $1/4$ of the tomato mixture. Repeat for the other 3 bowls.

Garnish with marjoram leaves and serve hot.

FRENCH TOAST

PREPARATION TIME : 10 MINUTES
SERVES : 4
(CONTAINS BREAD & MILK)

4 thick slices of bread	Halve the slices of bread.
1 whole egg 1 egg white 15 grams or 1 tablespoon sugar 3 tablespoons milk 3 tablespoons apple juice Salt to taste	Whisk together egg, egg white, sugar, milk, apple juice and a pinch of salt in a bowl. Dip the bread slices in this mixture till both sides are well coated.
2 tablespoons or 30ml melted butter	Heat butter in a frying pan and fry the soaked bread slices, turning sides, till both sides are evenly golden brown.
500 grams fresh mixed berries 4 teaspoons maple syrup	Serve the French toast with fresh berries and maple syrup.

CAFFEINE

(from left to right)

COLD BREW COFFEE

GREEK YOGURT WITH COFFEE FIG COMPOTE

Caffeine, is it really bad for you?

Caffeine, one of the many chemicals that coffee contains, has a beneficial effect on performance, as it is a stimulant that crosses the blood brain barrier and boosts concentration and mental alertness. It also stimulates cardiac muscle tissue, helps with fat loss and increases oxygen capacity. At the same time, excess consumption increases blood pressure, can cause headaches, sleeplessness and anxiety. It is not recommended to consume more than 4 cups of regular coffee per day. Never drink coffee on an empty stomach.

The type of coffee beans used, soil and climate where the beans are grown, the way in which the coffee beans are roasted and the way the coffee is prepared (filter or espresso) will influence the caffeine content. Dark-roasted beans will contain three or four times the amount found in a normal roasted one.

Caffeine is found in medicines, coffee, tea, chocolates, colas, several herbs like Guarana, Yerba, and Taurine.

When I was growing up coffee was synonymous with instant coffee or South Indian filter coffee. Today we have green coffee, ice coffee, espresso, French press, cold brew, drip and many others. The processing of coffee has become truly specialised with many techniques being used. Experiment a little!

POSITIVE TAKEAWAYS

+ Boosts concentration and mental alertness
+ Increases oxygen capacity
+ Excess causes anxiety and increases blood pressure
+ It accelerates fat loss

Caffeine contents of various drinks:

BEVERAGE/FOOD	QUANTITY	CAFFEINE (MG)
Coffee		
Filter	150ML	115
Expresso	60ML	100
Instant	150ML	60
Decaf	150ML	<1

Tea		
Black	150ML	30-50
Green	150ML	20-30

Chocolate Cake	1 slice	25
Red Bull	360ML	45
Coke/Pepsi	250ML	80
Pain reliever medicines	2 tablets	60-130

COLD BREW COFFEE

PREPARATION TIME : 20 MINUTES TO BREW
SERVES : 10-12
(LOW ACIDITY)

1 cup coarsely ground coffee powder
8 cups cold water

Note:
The ground coffee should have the texture of breadcrumbs. Any finer than that and you will risk getting cloudy, grimy-tasting coffee.

Put coffee powder in a jar and cover with cold water.

Stir gently until well combined, then cover and leave to brew, either in or out of the fridge for 18-24 hours.

When brewed, strain into a large bowl through a sieve to remove the grains of coffee.

Serve over ice, with or without milk and sugar (as per individual preference).

Cover and refrigerate the rest – it will stay good for a month or so due to the brew's low acidity.

Note:
Brew your cold-brew strong enough and you can even mix it with boiling water and serve it hot. This way the gentle, sweet flavours survive.

GREEK YOGURT WITH COFFEE FIG COMPOTE

PREPARATION TIME : 10-15 MINUTES

SERVES : 4

GF

- 1 cup brewed coffee
- 75 grams presoaked dried figs, chopped fine
- 1/2 teaspoon cinnamon powder
- 1/8 teaspoon green cardamom powder
- 1/8 teaspoon clove powder
- 1/8 teaspoon nutmeg powder
- 1 teaspoon orange zest

Heat together brewed coffee, figs, cinnamon powder, green cardamom powder, clove powder, nutmeg powder and orange zest in a non-stick pan.

Bring to a boil, reduce heat, cover and simmer for 3 minutes till the mixture is reduced to a syrupy consistency.

- 2 tablespoons honey (optional)
- 1 piece dark chocolate (optional)

Add honey, and chocolate, if required, and mix. Set aside to cool down to room temperature. Then cover and refrigerate.

- 700 grams plain Greek yogurt

Spoon 175 grams Greek yogurt into each of the 4 serving bowls. Top each generously with the coffee fig compote and serve.

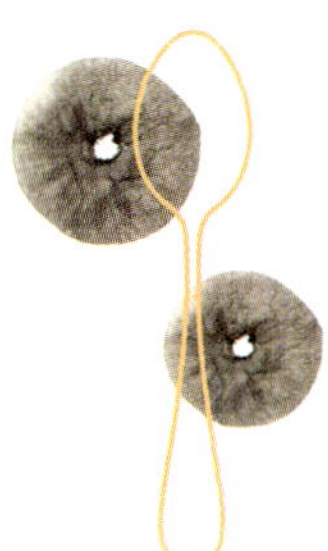

To brew coffee,
Take 1 teaspoon instant coffee and mix with 1/2 cup water or use the cold brew decoction brewed with freshly powdered roasted coffee beans.

Note : The properties of honey will change on cooking. If the coffee brew is very watery, then the syrup will not thicken easily. In such a case add sugar to thicken and avoid adding honey.

Optional : Add granola and muesli to have as a breakfast snack.

BARBECUED COFFEE SPICED CHICKEN

PREPARATION TIME : 20 MINUTES
SERVES : 3-4

GF

Coffee spice mix
- 1/4 cup finely ground coffee
- 1/4 cup brown sugar
- 2 tablespoons red chilli powder
- 1 tablespoon freshly ground black peppercorns
- 1 tablespoon paprika
- 2 tablespoons salt
- 1 tablespoon garlic powder
- 1 tablespoon onion powder
- 1/2 tablespoon cayenne pepper or chilli powder

- 2 tablespoons coffee spice
- 3 tablespoons olive oil

- 3 boneless chicken breasts

Mix all ingredients of the coffee spice mix. This mix can be stored for 3 months.

Spread olive oil in a baking dish. Sprinkle coffee spice on it and mix.

Pat the chicken dry and place it on top of the spice-oil mixture and mix. Make sure that the marinade coats the chicken breasts all over. Cover and keep the baking dish in the refrigerator and let the chicken marinate for about 1 hour.

Preheat the oven to 350°F/180°C.

Place the baking dish in the preheated oven and bake for 25-30 minutes.

Slice and serve hot.

COCOA CRUNCH SALAD

PREPARATION TIME : UNDER 10 MINUTES
SERVES : 4-6
(CONTAINS CHEESE)

4-5 cups cleaned greens (lettuce or other greens)
2-4 mandarin oranges, peeled and separated into sections
1-2 roasted or boiled beets, sliced
50gms feta cheese

Cocoa-Balsamic Vinaigrette

1 tablespoon olive oil
2 teaspoons balsamic vinegar
1 teaspoons cocoa powder
1/4 teaspoon ground cinnamon
1 teaspoons honey

---

2 tablespoons cocoa nibs
Sea salt
Coarse ground pepper

Layer the greens on a platter or salad plates. On top of the greens, arrange the oranges, beets, and cheese.

Combine all vinaigrette ingredients; stir or whisk thoroughly to blend in the cocoa powder and cinnamon.

Drizzle over the salad. Sprinkle cocoa nibs, salt, and pepper to taste. Serve immediately.

MENUS

VEGAN & GLUTEN-FREE

BREAKFAST

BUCKWHEAT CRÊPES

(WITH AVOCADO TURMERIC DIP) or

BERRIES, CHIA SEEDS OAT PARFAIT *or*

BANANA SLICES WITH PEANUT BUTTER

MID-MORNING

BEET & SPINACH JUICE

LUNCH

PUMPKIN & KALE SALAD *or*

QUINOA CHICKPEAS SALAD

COCONUT BASIL STIR-FRY

CHOCOLATE COCONUT BALLS

TEA

KALE FRITTERS

(WITH RIDGE GOURD PEEL CHUTNEY)

COLD BREW COFFEE

DINNER

BORSCHT

QUINOA PIZZA *or*

ZUCCHINI NOODLES

CARROT CAKE

EGG, DAIRY & NON-VEGETARIAN

BREAKFAST

AMARANTH OMELETTE *or*

KALE SALAD

(WITH MISO MUSHROOM OMELETTE) *or*

TOFU BHURJI *or*

RIDGE GOURD DOSA

(WITH RIDGE GOURD CHUTNEY)

MID-MORNING

SPIRULINA SMOOTHIE

LUNCH

KOKUM & BEET SALAD *or*

CARROT SALAD WITH FRESH TURMERIC

RATATOUILLE SHEPHERD'S PIE *or*

CHICKEN BLACK BEAN STEW

CHOCOLATE MOUSSE

TEA

SWEET POTATO WEDGES

(WITH RADISH PINE NUT DIP)

DINNER

LEAFY VEGGIE WRAP

(WITH RED PEPPER CILANTRO DRESSING)

SOBA IN TAHINI SAUCE *or*

ASIAN FISH CURRY

(WITH CAULIFLOWER RICE)

GREEK YOGURT WITH COFFEE FIG COMPOTE *or*

CARROT CAKE

GREENS

(Top Row: from left to right)
CORIANDER
PAKCHOY
LOLLO ROSSO

(Bottom Row: from left to right)
KALE
AMARANTH
ROMAINE LETTUCE

RECIPE INDEX

GLOSSARY

AGAVE	honey from the cactus flower
AMARANTH	rajgira
AMARANTH LEAVES	chawli patta
ARUGULA ROQUETTE	is a bitter leaf and is used mainly in salads
ASAFOETIDA	hing
SQUASH/PUMPKIN	kaddu/bhopla
CAYENNE POWDER/PEPPER	chilli powder/paprika
CHICKPEAS	kabuli chana
CILANTRO	coriander leaves
CORIANDER SEEDS	sabut dhania
COURGETTE	cucumber/zucchini
CUCRUMIN / TURMERIC	haldi
CUMIN	jeera
FENNEL / ANISE SEEDS	saunf
FENUGREEK SEEDS	methi dana
FLAX SEEDS	alshi
GARAM MASALA	mixture of spices like cardamom, clove, cinnamon etc
MUSTARD SEEDS	rai, sarson
PAPRIKA	spice from red capsicum. Red chilli powder is a good substitute
RADISH	mooli
RIDGE GOURD	torai
SHALLOTS	baby onions
SPRING ONIONS	hara pyaaz
SPIRULINA	is a naturally occurring blue-green micro-algae which grows in warm water alkaline lakes
SENNA	It is a laxative prepared from the dried pods of the cassia tree
SWEET POTATO	shakarkand, rattalu
YAM	jimikand, suran

Wheat : White wheat is devoid of the bran and the germ.

It is recommended that at least half of all grains consumed should be whole grains.

Bulgur : Wheat kernels are boiled, dried and cracked to get bulgur. It has more fibre than that found in quinoa, oats, millets and buckwheat. Since its fibre is soluble, it prevents constipation.

Bulgur is not the same as cracked wheat, which is not parboiled before it is cracked.

Durum : It is a variety of wheat that has a higher protein and gluten content than any other type of wheat and it is most often used in making pasta. Durum wheat products are not made from the whole kernel unless the package says "100 percent whole-grain durum". Most pastas are made from refined durum wheat flour.

Couscous : Contrary to popular belief it is not a grain but a kind of pasta made from semolina and wheat flour that is steamed.

Cornmeal : Finely ground corn grits. Polenta is coarsely ground grits.

Combine it with beans & legumes (refried beans) and tortillas.

Know your Rice

The most common varieties are typically classified by size and texture such as long, medium, and short-grained, and by the strain such as white, brown, red, black or purple There are also speciality rice, which include risotto and aromatic ones such as basmati, jasmine and japonica.

Not all rice created is equal

The nutritional value can vary depending on many factors including the type of rice, the soil the rice is grown on, if and how the rice is polished or processed, the manner in which it is enriched and how it is prepared before consumption.

After rice is harvested, the hull must be removed in order for it to be edible. If the rice is milled further, the bran and germ are removed, resulting in white rice, which is the kind of rice that most people eat.

The bran contains nutrients like protein, fat and dietary fibre and minerals. It also has immune building antioxidants.

Parboiled rice is rice that has been partially boiled in the husk, making it about 80 percent nutritionally similar to brown rice. It is high in fibre, calcium potassium and B6. This rice has lower glycemic index than white rice.

Brown rice contains protein, fibre and bran.

Black rice derives its rich colour from phytochemicals and antioxidants which are located in the inner portion of the rice bran. Just a spoonful of black rice bran contains more antioxidants than what are found in a spoonful of blueberries, but with less sugar and more fibre and vitamin E.

Red rice is a special variety of rice with a pleasant nutty flavour with an earthy tone. It derives its rich red from antioxidants. It has ten times the antioxidants of brown rice.

Long grain Basmati has a lower glycemic index than shorter grain rice.

Short grain is sticky when cooked.

Wild rice is not rice at all. It is a grain that grows wild and looks similar to rice.

Jasmine rice is a long grain variety of rice that has a subtle floral aroma and a soft, sticky texture when cooked. The grains are also shorter and thicker than Basmati rice. It has a high glycemic index.